ON HER OWN TERMS

ON HER OWN TERMS

Poems About Memory Loss
& Living Life to the Fullest

Carolyn Gammon

with quotations by Frances Firth Gammon

HARBOUR

Harbour Publishing Co. Ltd.
P.O. Box 219, Madeira Park, BC, VON 2HO
www.harbourpublishing.com

Front cover image by Carolyn Gammon
Edited by Silas White
Cover design by Carleton Wilson and Anna Comfort O'Keeffe
Text design by Carleton Wilson
Printed and bound in Canada
Printed on 100% recycled paper

Canada Council   Conseil des Arts
for the Arts   du Canada

Supported by the Province of British Columbia

Harbour Publishing acknowledges the support of the Canada Council for
the Arts, the Government of Canada, and the Province of British Columbia
through the BC Arts Council.

LIBRARY AND ARCHIVES CANADA CATALOGUING IN PUBLICATION

Title: On her own terms : poems about memory loss & living life to the fullest /
    Carolyn Gammon ; with quotations by Frances Firth Gammon.
Names: Gammon, Carolyn, 1959- author.
Identifiers: Canadiana (print) 20210246936 | Canadiana (ebook) 20210247029 |
    ISBN 9781550179651 (softcover) | ISBN 9781550179668 (EPUB)
Classification: LCC PS8563.A575 O5 2021 | DDC C811/.54—dc23

*I would like to dedicate this book to our elders
who face the challenge of memory loss.*

May your village be there for you.

Contents

Bright Margin of the Present

My mother can't recall
what was said two minutes ago

Not a big thing one would think
when we can chat, laugh, go for walks,
drink coffee, talk about the past
(if it's not too recent)

So why this existential threat,
gut-wrenching fear?
Fear it will spread to five minutes
yesterday
last year

Our remembered lives
disintegrate
quiet smouldering edge
paper slowly consumed
bright margin of the present
all that's left

I learn to speak in maybes
Perhaps I told you?
Were you there?
Let her direct the memories
not insist on mine

Learn to love her
for who she is
now
in case one day
I cannot offer her the pleasure
of a daughter's company

but only that of a warm hand

*I'm glad to know I have two daughters and I'm not in
heaven yet.*

Baby Pines

It started with baby pines
Family sitting at the cottage
Mum comments
casually enough
"Look at how many baby pines
there are this year!"

Twice in five minutes
same wording
same sentiment

"You said that five minutes ago,"
my sister points out

Perhaps if Mum had let it go
no one would remember that
as the first time
but she insisted, no
she had not noticed till now
the baby pines

Later she would learn
not to contradict
the younger minds,
would let things go

One of the baby pines has grown
shed needles and grown some more
provides cones for the fire

If I keep going downhill like this...
I'll climb a tree! Surprised you, didn't I?

Sending Me Home

"What's happening to me?
I wake at four and feel so fuzzy
What if Don dies?
Is he going to die?

I can't take it
He just lies there all day
What can we say to one another?
He should be in a home
hardly walks, feeble
I feel like I'm going off the edge
Please come"

Mum, I'll come in August

"I can't even imagine that far ahead
I don't know what's happening tomorrow"

Losing her memory
my mother may not remember this call
But I say: Yes I'll come

Jerk into action
make calls, arrange *things*
cancel commitments
spend money I earn in a season
for a plane ticket based on "imminent death"

Siblings advise
—she has to adjust—
adjust to his dying?

Arrange and arrange
Finally all is set
phone rings

Mum?

"I'm feeling better now
you don't have to come"

But Mum (I don't say)
there will be other four a.m.'s
he is dying
you are eighty-five

I'm happy to come!
(make it sound like a holiday)
How are the kittens?
"I don't know how many cats I have"
Don't worry about counting their paws
just their cute faces

Banter
counteracts four-a.m. fear
coursing through me
sending me home

I wish I were a nearer mother than a further mother.

In the Morgue

My mother's memory
dropped off the deep end
at my father's death

Stress and upset
factors of forgetfulness
even in the young

But he *had* died
and I *had* to tell her
hundreds and hundreds of times

"What are you up to Carolyn?"
Writing the program for Don's memorial
"Don's dead?
When did he die?
How did he die?"

A combination of illness
Diabetes, cancer, heart
Chose a different one each time
Spelled out his final days
A macabre game of snakes and ladders
back to square one

Each time the phone rang
made sure I answered
to tell the news
but one time, two weeks in
Mum picked it up
I heard her say
"Yes, Don's been ill
you can visit him in hospital"

Maybe it was one too many times
or the Gammon humour cracked its whip
I found myself yelling across the room
In the morgue Mum, in the morgue!

It didn't help
the doubt continued
A perverse Pinocchio
as if I were lying to her
just to be mean

Until it finally occurred to me
it's not that Mum can't remember,
it's that she doesn't want to know

Who died first, Don or I?

Stale

The house smells stale,
old, things decaying
even urine

Can't stand sleeping inside
choose a pull-out couch on the sun porch
keep the smell at a distance

Tell Mum: You should get out of this house
raccoons have nested in the back
New apartment is what you need!
New fresh new start

Some rooms are more oppressive than others
Sometimes the smells assault me:
wall of neglect, a family unable to care for its elders
Other times I have tea with Mum
don't notice the smells at all

It's four weeks after my father's death
I'm leaving my Mum "alone" she says
although my brother is in town
"It's not the same as a daughter"

On the plane, late over the Atlantic
rushing toward the sunrise
still hoping for elusive sleep
I grab my sweater to lean on

And there it is
that smell
stale
old

I cry
I miss it
so much

I am an orphaned mother.

Teetering

Trip before last
I saw my mother lug the laundry
down rail-less basement stairs
single light bulb
bad b-movie
couldn't see where she stepped

Back in Berlin I dreamt
Mum was teetering
on the top ridge of our house
I stood helplessly in the street
yelling for her to stay safe
unable to prevent her from falling

I'm not the premonition type
but it wasn't long
I was back
planning her move
from her home of fifty years

We prepped her best we could
talked it up
Close to downtown
view of the river
all meals included
like moving to the Hilton!

Day of the move
her best friend took Fran out and about
Lunch *and* supper! Trip to the mall!
What a day! What an excursion!
I doubt Mum thought of the move at all

By the time she arrived
at her new home
it looked like her old one!

Grannie Firth's writing cabinet
Aunt Sadie's love-worn carpet
family bookshelf
even her favourite tea service
All arranged neatly in one-tenth the space
For a moment Mum was moved
"It's beautiful!"

But when I went to leave
(bone-weary body and soul)
Mum said, "Take me with you
I want to go home"
Her beautiful room
out of sight, out of mind
No Mum, you live here now

The look she gave me
as if to say
not you too Carolyn

As bad as the time
we put Comet down

My mother always kept a calendar
"Buy yoghurt"
"Betty comes"
"UNB reunion"
To-do's of life
done gladly

The day she moved
she never noted another to-do

I fill my days wondering what I'm doing.

Fault Line

Once in Iceland
I stretched my arms
between the continental divide
Bumpy black igneous rock
tangible crevice

Going home
Coming home
always in between

My heart
a fault line between continents

Five time zones
Flying around the world
never landing
on the right spot

Aging mother needs her daughter
Preschool son needs his mother
I need both

Visits don't quite do it
each parting a little death
Crying on both ends
Always in between

Beneath the crevice
close to the surface
magma my conundrum

When are you coming to Canada?
Well, we will have a glorious reunion!

Mole Removal

"Now where are we going Carolyn?"
To the hospital to have that mole on your neck removed.
"Why does it have to be removed?"
You've been complaining about it for months Mum. Your shirt collar
    rubs it.
"Do I have to have it removed?"
It's been bugging you.
"Well, it's not bugging me now... So I won't have it done."

Mum, you wanted it done, you talked to the doctor yourself.
You're booked in today. Come on, let's go. Get your jacket on.
"Oh, do I have to?"
Yes Mum. Jacket.
"What jacket do I need?"
It's still cold—your winter jacket.
"My winter jacket? Where are my scarf and gloves?"
Here Mum.

"Now where are we going again?"
Mole Mum. Mole.
"What mole?"
The one on your neck that's been rubbing you.
"What do I have to have done?"
It has to be removed.
"Oh Carolyn, does it have to be today?"
Yes Mum.
"How did it come to this?"
It's just a mole Mum. You'll be in and out in ten minutes.
"Well, what jacket should I wear?"
Your winter one. Hurry now, we're going to be late.
"Where are my gloves and scarf?"
I have them here. C'mon.

"Oh Carolyn, I'm so confused."
You're doing fine Mum.
(Brushing her hair one last time, arranging her collar.)

"This mole on my neck is bothering me."
That's why we're going up to the hospital.
"The hospital!?"
It's your G.P. Mum, she does this sort of thing at the hospital,
not in her office.
"What sort of thing?"
Mole removals. Mole, mole, mole (singsong).
"Now, where are my…"
I've got them here Mum. Let's go, taxi's waiting.
(Leaving the room.)
"Oh Carolyn, what's to become of me?"
What do you mean?
"I mean living here. It's not home."
I know Mum but it's a lovely place.
Right downtown with a view of the river.
"I suppose you're right."
You couldn't stay alone in that big old house anymore Mum,
all by yourself… And here you get all your meals.
"The meals are lovely! … But you're all so far away.
I had a family of four and now you're all so far away."
I come home three times a year… from Berlin!
"I know and I appreciate that Carolyn, but I wish you were living here."
Sigh. Sigh.

(Frances sees the taxi and grabs her daughter's arm.)
"Now just tell me once more—where are we going?"
We're going up to the hospital.
"What for?"
You have to have your leg amputated Mum.
"You nut! I have to have that mole on my neck removed."
You got it Pontiac!
(To taxi driver) Hospital please.

When you're older you sprout moles.

22

Going Squirrelly

In my grandmother's day
if you lived long enough
memory loss was almost expected
"Going squirrelly" she called it

My child's mind
imagined Grannie's brain
like her extra hair buns
strategically placed under the net
a warm cuddly nest
allowing you to sit at home
knit and eat muffins
not have to partake
in the racy world outside

And if she dropped a stitch
we kept the booties anyway

By the time it was my mother's turn
seniors were to be active
in their golden years
Retirement full of travel
classes and condominiums
all those things one had postponed
raising children

Brain-boosting diets
antidepressants
memory games, vitamins

It seems there was no room left
for going squirrelly

My brain is on angels' wings.

Scandalous!

Why do people react as if it were a scandal
that I even contemplate having my elderly mother
with onset dementia live with me?

Wouldn't want to interrupt that unbridled independence
that holiday, that dinner for two
It might affect your work! Your salary!
Your free time!

You are naive!
You can't do it!

Family says no
Therapist counsels against it
Friends say, Are you joking?

Only one person, my partner
says, Try. It might be hard, but try
Thank you Katharina

What I want to know is this:
Can these well-intentioned advisors
imagine themselves old and in need?

In a world turned on its head
Career, independence, money
all more important
than an aging mother
stumbling block

Scandalous
to consider caring for my mother in

How could I?

You are such a loyal little daughter.

Sandwich

In the shallow waters of Grand Lake
one hand my five-year-old son
fluorescent orange water wings
eager to swim, swim, swim
one hand my eighty-five-year-old mother
fragile but eager too, still able to swim

I wonder if I let go
who will I have to save first?

When Noel was very little
those precious cottage times
I could put the two together
Mum would read aloud
her clear, expressive librarian's voice
stories about giants or Amelia Bedelia

But all too soon the eighty years between them
meant little common ground
though even as a teen
Noel would roast marshmallows with Grannie
and once in a shopping mall
he took off with Mum in her wheelchair
to play hide-and-seek

It is that summer on the cusp
I feel the sandwich most keenly
By next summer, my son can swim
my mother needs water wings

Money spent to commute overseas
my son does not have for a new bike
Money spent on a school trip tips the scales
I cannot make the spring visit to Canada

I am a thick piece of cheddar
between the two
trading off time and energy
one for the other

I feel my son tugging at my arm
He wants to swim on his own wings
I feel my mother tugging at my arm
She wants to float on her back

I release them both and plunge
under the cool
golden-brown waters of Grand Lake

Upon hearing buzz flies at the cottage:
Could you turn that sound down please?

No Withdrawals

Mum paid rental car and gas
one August her Visa expired
Agent on the phone asks to speak to her

"1918" I hear her say
Good Mum! Go for it!
"Current prime minister?"
Silence

Another moment
at the doctor's office
I speak of family needs:
could Mum sign a few documents?
The kind doctor has known her for years
looks me in the eye
sad smile says it all
You know…
We all know…
your mother
mustn't sign things now

We never did the tests
never had Mum declared
the word we couldn't say

Credit card agent, doctor
let us know
It's over now
no more signatures
no withdrawals

I find forgetting easy.

Burning at Both Ends

My mother
a candle
burning at both ends

The one end
short-term memory
like a fuse growing shorter
Ten minutes, five, two

"Did we pay the bill?"
Yes, you paid yourself
"Did we pay the bill?"
Yes, you gave a nice tip
Different answers
to the same questions
keep us all entertained

The other end
long-term memory
disappearing from the present backwards
"Did Ross ever marry?"
He married five years ago Mum

But she stills defines arcane words
corrects my grammar
(though I think my grammar's good)
And her wit, a warm welcome wind
infuses every conversation

"Now let me repeat myself"
No! Don't! Bite your tongue!
"I've bitten it off already
I'm talking through my nose"

Once, we brought bikes up from the basement
wondered if she'd remember how
Off over the trails of Fredericton
body remembering what mind may not
"I'd love to go on another bike trip!"
Plans for the future
where memory is not needed

This memory loss
hardening of the arteries
we called it a generation before
doesn't just take away
Gathering rocks on the beach
Mum finds heart-shaped ones
as if in a field of four-leaf clover

Running her E.T. fingers over
a rose quartz heart
she says with a laugh
"I'm a lone petunia in an onion patch"
asks after my family in Berlin
still by name

I am getting stranger as I grow older.

A Love Poem for Your Ninetieth Year

I love you
for giving Jen and me words and ideas
Every night after supper
we sat on two big juice cans
in front of the kitchen blackboard
"Mum, Mum, tell us something to draw!"
"Draw a castle, a peacock, a sunset..."
Every time you were to judge
"Who won Mum? Whose is the best?"
In your judicial way
you kept two little red-headed, pigtailed girls from fighting
"This time Jennifer but yours is imaginative too Carolyn"
As you did dishes after serving a supper for seven
you entertained us, evening for evening
Your love, rock strong
playful as the grey squirrels
tightroping power lines past the kitchen window

"Chicken... and dressing... and cranberry sauuuccceee!"
I'd yell dashing full speed down the hall
spring into your arms, my scrawny legs wrapping round your hips
You'd hold my hands, I'd dangle backward
my face to yours and the ceiling
"My turn! My turn!" Jen would yell and run
"Chicken... and dressing... and cranberry sauuuccceee!"
Over and over till your arms must have been sore
as we got older and heaver, it must have been a strain
I love you for catching me
again and again and again

In the backyard, evening badminton games
you'd make a foursome with Peter, Jen and me
playing into the twilight till we no longer saw the bird
Still we begged you to stay for another game
You always hid your age
because you were six years older than Don

but when I look back now, you were mid-fifties
playing badminton into the dusk as if you were twelve like me
I love you for not telling your age

I loved you at the cottage
when you'd bathe us in the zinc tub
take us girls by the hand to the outhouse
because we were afraid of ghosts
When you lay tanning, Jen and I would sneak up
tickle you with long thin grass tips
You'd not open your eyes but shoo away the flies
as if you didn't know flies don't giggle
Or we'd place stones all over your back
so you'd wake with a Dalmatian tan
and you pretended not to notice
I love you for pretending

I never minded being sick home from school
If one of us was sick, you'd keep the other sister home for company
We'd eat Mr. Christie's arrowroot cookies dipped in milk
watch *The Friendly Giant* or *Captain Kangaroo*
Being sick was fun and you were always there
I love you for being there

When Peter had his accident
you kept Jen and me out of school alternate days
to keep him company in hospital
You understood that in the long run
a few math formulas more or less
should not keep sisters from being there for their brother
I love you for your good sense

One of my first memories, I am maybe three or four
Jen goes crooked on the wooden swing
splits my head open
screaming in pain, blood streaming down my face
I see you running toward me in the backyard
In hospital the doctor applied ether to my nose and mouth

I held your hand and knew I'd be all right
I love you for comforting me

Scared at night like any little kid by times
you'd always come when I called
I remember you'd calm me and say:
"I'll be right back," and go away
In that magical space of time
when you'd be right back
I'd slip away to sleep
Forty years later I use those words with my son:
"I'll be right back"
I love you for coming when I called

When Jen started school, I had kindergarten mornings
Being the last child meant a special afternoon
alone with you for a whole year
I don't recall what we did Mum
it was so specially ordinary
but then you'd lay me down to rest
with my favourite pile of 45s
"Jamaican Farewell" repeating as I woke
I love you for making me feel special
alone with you, cozy and safe

When the boys brought animals home
snakes, salamanders, chippies and squirrels
Mathew the raccoon, Buckwheat the crow
a snapping turtle for a winter in the back bathtub
a boa constrictor moved into the dining room
a tarantula arrived in the mail...
You took it all in stride
as our house transformed into Noah's ark
When Geoff moved out—who fed the boa?
Who kept the world's oldest gerbil alive?
When you reached into the potato sack and pulled out a garter snake
you simply said, "Tell Peter I found his snake"
When Ratty got out and ended up on your pillow at night

you gently returned her to her cage
I love you for allowing us a zoological childhood

We had no housework
Four able-bodied children and you did it all
I stood in the warm space between stove and wall
watching you cook, seldom offering a hand
You spoiled us and made our childhood a holiday
for the boys and girls alike
I love you for giving us a childhood free of housework
When I moved out on my own
went to make a pie, I crimped the edges
just like you did, poked it five times round
I realized how much you taught without teaching
as I stood there by the warm stove

I don't remember learning to read
but I do remember you reading to me
and maybe I learned because you didn't insist
and osmosis is the best teacher

I love you for bringing your mother to live with us
Grannie's room was the best room of the house
full of sewing supplies, hairpins and patience
Grannie was an old angel
seventy-eight when I was born
yet a strong kind presence
Her rabbit coat hung behind the door was soft like her love
and when she needed care, you cared for her
I never forgot that lesson
one of the most important

You couldn't sing but loved to hear us sing
"Down, down the River St. John"
"They built the ship *Titanic*, to sail the ocean blue"
If you tired of our same songs
every car trip, you never said so
always praised our chirping

as if we were opera stars in training
My drawings, scrapbooks, my little creativities
you took each as a gift
I love you for giving me room to unfold
your love like an origami swan
intricate, delicate, beautiful

I loved the desserts you made to bring sweetness into our lives
frozen ambrosia, angel food cake with boiled icing
apple crumble, chocolate mocha pudding
Your turkey dinners were second to none
leftovers just as good as the first time round
I wasn't so keen on tongue but we were a family of seven
on one income and you rarely made us feel it
I love you for cooking the foods I loved

Most of all Mum
I love your humour
Even in these last years
when maybe there are less things to laugh about
You make your wry comments
don't let a chance go by without a twist of meaning
A pun, a spoonful of humour to help the medicine go down
They say humour is a family trait
If so, then I have your genes
Mum, I love you for making life laugh

Mothers don't last forever.

Wild Pearl

With thanks to Betsy Warland for the inspiration
and the courage to tell the backstory

Everyone praised me
such a wonderful daughter
an example, a martyr!
But there's a backstory

I loved my in-house grannie
as only a little girl could
unreservedly
no strings attached
pure love
She was gentle
She was kind
She was tolerant
She sewed and knit
ate muffins and drank tea
like a grannie should

She took us girls to the Fredericton Ex
paid our rides and cotton candy
held our hands on the Ferris wheel

For our part
Jen and I helped her with church bazaars
gathering second-hand goods for the needy
A fair exchange

Grannie was a soft rock
Her room
an oasis
in a chaotic, sometimes brutal house

Grannie always kept her hair in buns
made from her own hair

She didn't look grey even at ninety
Soft pads of hair, decades old
adjusted just so
under a fine net

Once in a while I saw her combing
her hair with an ivory brush
for a salt shampoo
but soon it was up again in orderly fashion
securely held by bobby pins, the invisible net

Until one day, perhaps I was fourteen
paramedics carried Grannie downstairs
her hair flung wildly round her shoulders
Who was this wild woman
with her hair so strewn?

That was the beginning of back and forths
hospital and homes
Broken hips and decubitus ulcers
known as bedsores
Those tender places
where the skin reds and wrinkles
tissue-paper soft
then breaks through

I was a teen
How dare my grannie be sick!
I felt betrayed
Refused to visit her
in hospital or a home
even if my mother and sister did
I stayed in the car
That was not my grannie
not that one with the wild hair
No, I wouldn't visit a strange woman

Until the day
Mum said ironically
"Well, she can just as well break a hip at home"
And Grannie came home again

She wasn't the same
She could barely hold a conversation
let alone a knitting needle
We had to turn her in bed
on a regular basis
"It's your turn to turn Grannie, Jen!"
"No, it's your turn!"

But at least her hair was done up
Mum must have seen to it
And sometimes we had funny conversation
snippets where she sounded like herself

Once, sitting up, she told me of tiny pearls
she'd found in clams on the Escuminac Flats
wild pearls
Had them set in a crescent moon
I knew the brooch
Now I knew the story
Yes, this tiny story was still
very much essence-of-Grannie

She still liked muffins and tea
though sometimes ate the napkin by mistake

I was eighteen
when it was too much for my mother
and Grannie returned to the home
for the last time
It was before remote-control beds
before they knew the elderly had to be upped
whether they could themselves or not
"mobilized" it's called today

Before air-pocket mattresses
that cradled fragile old bones

And so one day my friend Nicole
in nursing at UNB asked,
"Is your grandmother Mrs. Firth?"
Yes, why?
"We visited the home today
Your grandmother was shown to us
—the worst case of decubitus ulcers
they had ever seen"

Something broke inside me
It has never repaired

My beloved grandmother
My hair bun, hair net, orderly grannie
my oasis, gentle-voiced Grannie Firth
"the worst case of decubitus ulcers
they had ever seen"

I was on a basketball trip in Calgary
Family didn't even tell me she had died
They thought it would upset me so

But I swear, something grew in me
something hurt that needed fixing
something strong and sure
like a wild pearl

I would be there for my mother

*I'd like your macabre poetry well enough Carolyn,
if it weren't about the family!*

Tsunami

You've lost four years in a blip
Painstaking weeks, months
learning to live in a "new home"

"This is no way to handle me
take me from my home to this strange place!"

Dear Mum that happened four years ago
not today

"Well, you can see how loony I've become"
You're not loony, you've just blown a gasket

Over the phone from Berlin
I have her take an album off the shelf—
Tell me what you see
"Here's one on a beach… let me see, it says,
'Scattering Don's ashes'—so he is really dead?"

What strange chemistry has sliced off a chunk of your life
cliff falling into the sea

Do you recognize where you are?
"I've never been here before—I need to go home"
I moved you four years ago
"But what happened to all my things?"
They're in your room
"What room?"

Just this summer you swam in Grand Lake
Celebrated your ninetieth
Everyone remarked how well you're doing
Just today with help you sent me an email

"Here's another photo… It's a grave
Funny, there seems to be a spot of light
where the second date should be
I see myself reflected in the stone
where the date should be"

Do I love you too much?
Maybe I'm not letting you go
holding you here with my love grip
Can't stand the thought of not hearing your voice
next visit to look forward to
With sheer willpower across the ocean
I hold you to this earth
as the moon does the tides

"If my mind is going to be this whacky
I don't want to live"

You still know my name
"Is that enough?"
At this moment it's enough for me.

Very strange
On the one hand you are four years erased
On the other, your present
is sharper than it has been in years

Instead of memory you have a magnifying glass
You tell me it was just Remembrance Day
tell me about Geoff's girlfriend
when you never could remember her before
You speak with energy and vehemence
candidly about life and death

as if a tsunami has flooded your brain
then withdrew, leaving wreckage and dead
but also a few bright flowers
struggling up through the swamp
to the sun

I feel as confused as a rat in a mouse hole.

Should I Fly?

You're in pain
I'm thousands of miles away

Not how you imagined your end-of-life

Four children, where are we now
the moment of your worst fears?
Moments of abandonment
rising to the surface of a well-prepared life
For years now I have spent every cent I own
and some I don't to visit and care for you
My year's rhythm your heartbeat

I swore as a child I would care for you in your old age
and I've done it
I've flown time and again
helped you uphold friendships
guided your pen to write Christmas cards
dictated your diary
slept over, a mattress on the floor
so we could sing old camp songs
so you might sleep that one night in perfect contentment
wake to see me there
I've cared for you at the cottage
helped you dress, take meds
soaked your feet and hands, manicures, pedicures
rubbed lotion on your anatomically astounding body
your legs like the worlds' river system
"These legs could be used in the science lab at UNB"
We jest to cover the too-intimate moments
bodily duties you'd rather do yourself
How many old albums have we labelled together?

I threw you a hell of a ninetieth birthday party
What more can I do?

"When are you coming?"
I hesitate
"When are you coming?"
I know it means I love you

Every moment I'm not there
is a moment less of our lives together
You were forty-one when I was born
I've been lucky to have you so long
"Am I ninety!?"
This questionable miracle

I want to hold your hand, ease your pain
be the daughter I promised

You're in pain
Do I book the next flight?
Drop my life in Berlin like a cold pancake
or save the panic, the money I do not have
for the next time?

Should I fly Mum?
Should I fly?

I don't know why you chose Germany...
it has such an anti feel about it.

Together

They tell family it won't be long
Eight thousand kilometres between us sisters
We arrive in Fredericton the same day

Together we care for Mum
Together we laugh and cry
I'd forgotten your powerful humour Jen
as you make a dead chicken out of a towel
We're in stitches with Mum at death's door

We use the time
when not in that close intimacy of the sick room
to walk the old train bridge
river ice breaking beneath us
say where the ashes would be strewn

So good not to be alone
have someone else to help make decisions
not just someone, a sister

Mum is down to one waking hour a day
We prop her up in bed
As always she does her best
smiling wanly, trying to sip tea
wondering why we hover with such concern

The day before Mum would have died
—she couldn't draw water through a straw—
It's you Jen who says this can't be right
It's me who makes the call
"Our mother is being drugged to death"
The extramural nurse cancels morphine
Within hours Mum is back on earth

Sitting up now in her easy chair
dusty rose housecoat

matching the new rose in her cheeks
thin for a thin woman
Mum enjoys her celebrated status
reads a poem with melodramatic flare
tilts her head gallantly for a photo
clasps our hands as dearly as we do hers

Like a boxing match where no one lost
we all rejoice
together

I am still clinging to the vine.

Saving Your Life

Mum! We saved your life
At the forty-second kilometre of your drug marathon
called off the killer meds

Enough drugs to down a bull it seemed to us
For days I cannot get a doctor on the phone
let alone to make a house call
Though you are over ninety
with compression fractures
cannot rise from bed

Well-intentioned caregivers,
nurses—a new one each day—
and your loving family
administer morphine

Then watch you day by day
dying on drugs

One more day
you would have been gone

Already you could not sit unaided
open your eyes
We became used to that
It was when you could no longer swallow
that Jennifer and I panicked

This nurse was different
came in person
looked askance at your med sheet
"It looks like Hitler's war plan in the last days"

Asks why you are being wakened from pain-free sleep
to be given fast-acting morphine?

As if you were acutely injuring yourself every four hours
Why extra-strength Tylenol for a man thrice your size?

Everyone was just following orders

This nurse dares to contradict her colleagues
Off *all* painkillers!
Give only when requested by patient

Supposedly Mum, you were bedridden and dying
yet within six hours of the last morphine
you walk down the corridor without aid
Within twenty-four hours you are joining the others for night lunch

I ask the nurse who made the difference
How did she know?
Her own father, she told me, had almost died this way
He's still alive, years later...

I am overjoyed!
Angry too, but mostly relieved and joyful
I savour every step you take back to life
Two nights after near-death
we attend a concert together
A week later you walk a mile by my side

Late at night I cannot sleep
thinking about you Mum
Dependent on help
living in a home you did not choose
No short-term memory
Can't do activities so dear to you
A writer and reader all your life
you can do neither now
You enjoy my visits
but have no memory of them

I know you never wanted to live like this

What lies ahead?
More compression fractures, more pain
Eventually a death like this one you almost had
on morphine, but the next time, for real?

Should we have let you go Mum?
Unnaturally like this
This modern form of euthanasia

We did not make a conscious decision
We acted on instinct as daughters should
We saved your life, and now

I shouldn't be out here; I don't believe in heaven.

Lazarus

I am so happy
Mum is alive!

As the river ice was freeing itself
first floes breaking out of the mass
She broke free of a morphine death

"What's wrong with me?" she asked
You have a bad back, we said
though it didn't make sense
"What's wrong with me?"
she asked again and again
until finally it occurred to us
she was not just repeating herself

You don't die from a bad back
even at ninety

It took courage
to come back to life at that last hour
She had not walked in weeks
Family came to let her go

But the river heaved
outside her window
the first squirrels de-hibernated
icicles dripping
when she rose and walked a mile

We called her Lazarus

This summer
wild roses bloomed on the beach
swallows dashed to their round holes
under the cottage eaves

We went out every day on the lake
Mum talked of her childhood
on the Restigouche River
the big Gaspé canoe

No repetitive questions
No meds, no death in sight
just blue lake and sparkles
We took a break on a faraway stony beach
sipped apple juice, shared a power-bar

The photo shows us windblown and happy
Lazarus and her daughter

I have peace in my ear.

A Place That Has Always Been

My mother time-travels
on a regular basis

By moments
she is a debonair graduate of UNB
ready to face the world
intently bent over archival papers
with Eleanor, loving the work
She recognizes photos of Don the grad
but not grown-old

Age does not exist
in her young mind
I am not over fifty, no no
I am the spirited redheaded
adventuresome girl she has always known

Mum was once a stickler for time
sourpuss mood
if I was a few minutes late
She was once a travelling
companion of a wealthy cousin
Vietnam! Barbados! Tierra del Fuego!
Now, time and travel are measured
not in minutes and miles
but in leaps of the mind

It is not always fun

Mum wakes from a nap
"Are my parents alive?"
I calculate quickly…
Your father died over sixty years ago…
"And Mother?"
Over thirty years ago

Flustered and annoyed
"Then what's the use of living?"

I take her hands
help swing her legs
to the edge of the day sofa
talk about tea and carrot cake
Tell her, We're here, Mum
We're here at the cottage

Chipmunks and jays
brown orange beach stones
loons in flight
flying grasshoppers
crickets at night

Away from the nursing home
a place that has always been

(About the cottage)
Our little pearl in the woods.

Into Transparency

The Talmud says
if you save one life
you save the world

I believe if you save memories of one life
you save the world of the mind

Every week we save your world
the textures of your voice and mine
key words, intonations, names
complementary meanings
cottage, Don, Betty, home, fiddleheads
Campbellton, UNB, four children

"My grandfather"
conjures up a large-moustached man
Henry Dove Frost Troop
portly and kind, baby Frances on his knee
a coveted only child

We both see a veranda
overlooking the gentle Annapolis River
It's 1919, lace-up boots and wooden pitchforks
sea of white pink apple blossoms

Synapses neurotransmitting
Tangible as the agate you found on the Escuminac Flats
polished and set in silver
Not a diamond, not an opal
this plain agate, your favourite stone

Every week we sail the opaque ocean
brown land and green waters
bringing our worlds
into transparency

When did you and I start travelling together?

All Dressed Up and Nowhere to Go

"Saturday night and I ain't got nobody..."
—Sam Cooke

My Mum doing the death reach
an arm broken to fragments
actively dying on morphine

From this brink we thought
she would never come back

For weeks, months, Mum lived in hospital
in johnny shirts
humiliating tailored sheets tied at the neck
In her case, one arm dangling

Johnny shirts are good for staff
washing a bedridden patient

Mum found her own way back
No drug, no doctor, no daughter from Germany
She did it herself
One day we were no longer worried
that each day would be the last

But still the johnny shirts persisted

Living in hospital it was the only garb available
I started taking Mum on excursions
wheeling her out of her room
down the hall, the next hall, the next

I'd dress her up in her cuddly housecoat
but she felt uncomfortable in "public" undressed
I put pants on her, a sweater to hide the johnny shirt

Then, I started to help her dress
Even if late in the afternoon, I'd take the time
socks, pants, undershirt, blouse
Leave the johnny shirt behind
Elevator down to the cafeteria
Takeout coffee and homemade hospital muffins
We looked like… visitors!

Every day I'd wheel Mum in front of the nurses' station
See? She's dressed… no more johnny shirt!

Mum began eating by herself
using her broken arm to lift the spoon
taking a few steps with help
thinking of a life outside

In the hospital chapel I'd make two rows of chairs
Supporting herself on both sides
Mum walked between them five yards, ten yards
Touchdown! Mum can walk!

Then came the day I arrived in mid-afternoon
There was Mum sitting up in her chair
fully dressed
smiling like the Cheshire Cat!
I broke into tears
We celebrated with Dunster's donuts and coffee
Mum held the cup herself

One day I added beads, earrings
that bit of rouge

I abducted her, took her OUT
downtown to the Green
She walked on damp grass
sat on a real wooden bench
hair tossed in a pulsing wind
We ate at the Beaverbrook Hotel

She forgot she was living in the hospital

Then I had to fly back to Germany
the life I neglect when I'm not neglecting Mum
When I'm not here no one takes her out
Her own friends are elderly
Her son cannot do her personal care en route
She's fragile
No one dares it seems

I call my mother frequently
She sounds so chipper
I ask her if she's dressed
Yes, yes, she has her dark purple sweater on today
the one Patty gave her for her birthday
She sounds so alive, so ready

All dressed up and nowhere to go

I hope I don't die and am not able to wear my new clothes.

Blowing Her Nose

Have you ever helped someone
blow her nose from overseas?

New Brunswick lacks nursing home rooms
so Mum lives in hospital

We're on the phone
chat pep talk storytelling banter
Mum interrupts "I have to blow my nose"
Can you see the tissues? I ask
"I can see them, but I can't reach them"
Bars on Mum's bed prevent her from falling
prevent her from reaching the tissues

I tell my Mum to hang up
I call the nurses' station
…would someone mind…

Call Mum again
She is happily blowing her nose
sipping an evening power drink

I wonder how many times
her nose is running
and no one is calling from overseas

I am unbearably comfortable.

The Little Cyclist

A lifelong cyclist
Mum never lost the thrill
Spiffy that last ride
sunset orange jacket
racing-stripes helmet
feet in rat traps like a pro

The next home
I brought her a little cyclist
eight inches high
With a flick of a switch
he pedalled away
legs pumping, lights flashing
along the waxed buffed corridors

Mum loved the little cyclist
following in her wheelchair
wherever he went
she never passed
politely let him lead the way
Homecare workers
smiled to see the little cyclist
round a corner, knowing Frances
would be on his heels

One time we all travelled together
the little cyclist, Mum and I
talking about road trips with Kay
Magdalen Islands, Rocher Percé
waterproof panniers packed with snacks
"PEI is more hilly than I thought!"
"A hard day's journey"

The little cyclist hit a bump and fell
Must have a flat, we said
I righted him and on we went

corridor after corridor
dining room pond aquarium
nurses' station, civilization
Wheeled and gabbed heart to heart
waved at passersby
until at last the little cyclist headed home

Home, home
to the room with photos of Frances and family
"Look! That's me!"
delighted to be back

That evening
Mum asked me to write a letter for her
"Dear Father, I've been away on a trip
I know I promised not to be gone long
Carolyn is such a good companion"

The little cyclist
on his kickstand within view
Frances speaks of roads she's travelled

Who's to say
we're not relaxing after fifty K
That Frances had not been to Rocher Percé
that day?

I am not exactly kicking up my heels,
but I am moving them along the floor.

Good Days Bad Days

Another late-night call to Berlin
my brother Geoff
"Mum's fallen again
broken her other arm
gashed her head
blood on her brain"
Within forty-eight hours
I'm at her side

Each fall, each broken bone
diminishes her
This time she is bent
irretrievably it seems to the side
away from the broken arm
A human pretzel

Looks like she's been hit by a baseball bat
Her head stitched, thin skin multicoloured
the "wheeling wounded" we joke

There are good days and bad days

On good days
Mum can raise her head
keep her eyes open
hold a cup of tea herself
enjoy a new German teddy
or a kitty brought by Marion

On bad days
Mum is not comfortable
groans, fusses the blankets
eyes glued shut
Supper is two mouthfuls
I find unchewed hours later

Good days
she says something coherent
on the phone to an old friend
On a bad day
I ask if she wants to talk to Betty
She says, "No"

A good day she recognizes
"O Canadaaaa" on the piano
A bad day we do not leave her room
for the piano down the hall

A good day she picks up the fork herself
A bad day she cannot find her mouth

A good day she does exercises on command
"Wiggle your toes, lift your leg"
A bad day she cannot will her toes to wiggle

A good day she calls me Carolyn
A bad day she does not speak

We all have good days and bad days
but with the very elderly
it is a matter of life
or not

Heal me before I drop dead.

A Joke on Her Lips

You're lucky you're not Shiva
I jest with Mum after recovering
from seeing her battered by the latest fall
You have no more arms to break
"I still have my legs"
Mum says wryly

She bit her tongue going down
When I give her mashed chicken for lunch
she winces, "That chicken bit me!"

I think humour
may be the last thing
to go

All bones will have been broken
all indignities complete
I think she will die with a joke on her lips

The best one of all

A pastor arrives
asks my secular mum
if she may pray with her
Always polite, Mum says yes

The pastor kneels at my mother's bedside
joins hands like a steeple
"Are you listening Lord?"
A measured, resonant voice emanates
deep from within the bedcovers
"Yes, I am listening!"

The pastor, somewhat bewildered
explains the situation to God
"This woman has broken *her arm*!"

The voice acknowledges
picking up the cadence
in the pastor's earnest plea
"Yes, she has broken *her arm*!"

The pastor hesitates
looks slowly around the room
then mustering her wits
continues stalwartly
"I want you to *heal* this woman!"
A rich sonorous voice
emphatically asserts
"I will *heal* her!"

The pastor's cheeks are glowing
I bow my head, cough, stave off hysterics

Neither of us know
if the laudanum is speaking
if we just witnessed a channelling
of Frances the Lord

Or was it simply Mum
wanting that one last joke?

You have to be witty when you're lying flat on your back.
You've got to have something.

With Me, Knowing Me

It's been a hard visit
You're more scattered
introduce me as your sister
talk about me, to me, in the third person

Bodily functions take up most of the day
chewing, resting, visiting the bathroom
hardly leaves time
for those precious quality-of-life moments

Still we valiantly *do* things as before

Choose a quiet corner of your favourite restaurant
you doze over puréed fish chowder
At the Christmas market you barely raise your head
to see the pretty things
Look Mum! Look! I feel like a five-year-old
Meet an old acquaintance
but even the social graces
you were once so good at are elusive

We do your Christmas cards
I want friends and family to see your handwriting
know that Frances is still Frances
Takes perseverance
letters disappear, grow smaller
tilt sideways off the page
Writing on the bending bough of a willow
You practise, write big, in pencil, erase, try again
I trace your words in ink
downsize to hide the faults
A pastoral note from Frances, Merry Christmas

Phone calls are booby-trapped
Simple questions you cannot answer about yourself
embarrassing silence on the other end

Non-sequiturs, cul-de-sac
On speakerphone I interject
but soon the conversation is mine, not yours

Every day I arrive at the home is a surprise
yanking you out of your inner world
"Where did you spring from?!"
as if I've dropped in from an alien planet

Till now I've always kept the spirit
It is the first visit I falter
And it is coming to an end

I have made a memory album
Together Again, December 2010
"That rhymes," you say

Today when I arrived you were sitting up
reading a *Peanuts* book for old times' sake
We laugh! Tell Gammon jokes
Enjoy the album sitting in the soft beams of a winter sun

If only I could hold you in my mind like that today
pink and orange rays
you, comfortable, happy
with me, knowing me

Soon some of them, like myself, will be dead
and I won't have to send so many cards.

Frances and Katharina

Katharina comes home with me
each summer to Canada
My beautiful extraordinary life partner
Afro-German historian, activist, author
honorary New Brunswicker

Mum calls her "Kathi"
a name reserved for family in Heidelberg
and Mum
They always got along
"She has such a beautiful smile"
Mum says again and again
"Your mother has such wit"
Katharina says
Both historians, educated women
They share their love for
me!

We arrive at Mum's care home
one sunny August afternoon
It's been over a year
Mum's not in her room
Katharina finds her first
in the common room
I witness their meeting

"Kathi!"
Mum's joyous smile of recognition
stronger than the sun
beaming on lime-green walls
Katharina smiles too
her award-winning cross-ocean smile

Mum gathers Katharina's broad hand
into her two long veined ones
Won't let go
a long-lost friend
found again

Memory of a good woman
inventing scrumptious meals
behind the cottage counter
Playing her accordion
in the big German beach chair
Walks on the Green
between daughter
and daughter-in-law

Memory as warm as a wind
from around the point

Frances has won the memory lotto

I hope you have some sparks that shine through at my age.

Cottage Nursing Care

Mission impossible
"You could earn a lot of money doing this Carolyn"

Getting ready for bed takes an hour
Stand up, pants down, sit down, pants off
pine-green flannel pyjamas
"I *love* these pyjamas Carolyn
Did you get them for me?"
Yes Mum, your *haute couture* comes from Berlin
PJs on, stand up, PJs up, sit down
Teeth time: No Mum don't use that water!
Cottage water hasn't been tested, here's your glass
Rinse three times, floss
Have you ever tried to floss someone else's teeth?
Brush, rinse again (No! Not that water!)
Isn't that a nice clean feeling?
Switch wheelchair to walker to toilet
six-foot-square space
Toilet to walker to wheelchair
Cream feet
Your feet are in great shape Mum!
"I am spoiled with wellness"

Off to the bedroom
Katharina lifts Mum's legs
I swivel her upper body
pillow under the calves so heels don't rub
Heaven forbid that her daughter cause bedsores
Meds, eye drops, more cream
One last check, unwrinkle PJs
or I will see those wrinkles imprinted on her back
ten hours later

In case she wakes and wonders where she is
I sleep beside her
In the night I see a Grecian profile

If I cannot hear her breathe
I think: That's it
This is what it will be like
in the end
solidified sleep

Next morn all systems reverse
I support Mum from behind
Katharina swivels legs
No matter how gently
after hours of immobility
Mum's Quasimodo back
pain, pain, pains
I'm sorry Mum! Sorry Mum!
Sorry, sorry, sorry!

Moments between bed and wheelchair
Doubt invades
Is it right?
Should I have brought Mum to the cottage
again this year?
No remote-control perfect-tilt bed
No nurse nearby

Sometimes she asks looking out the bay window
"What body of water is this?"

But this is not the moment to doubt
I massage life back into her back
coax and cheer, and she makes it…
to the edge of the bed!
Two-person transfer
lift, pivot, swoop
she's up for the count!

Morning ablutions
sticky sweet astronaut drink
up down up down

brush and spit, cream and rub
I spread a warm washcloth across her back
"Oh Carolyn, that feels soooo good!"
Fresh undershirt, her fave crimped cotton blouse
stripes of lime-green soft yellow cottage colours
meds, glasses, clip-on earrings
just for fun

An hour has gone by
six square feet of space
when I yell to the main room for a drum roll

To Mendelssohn's bridal chorus she appears
"Here comes the mum!"

Frances eyes the fire in the hearth
made especially for her though a bright sunny day
"What a BEAUTIFUL fire!"

*The nice thing about lying down is
you can forget about other parts of your body.*

Playing Dolls

I never liked playing dolls
too girly, borrrr-inng
those stiff-legged plastic-faced
lifeless beings

Never liked the tools of the female trade
but Frances did, her cosmetics box
full of flip-top powder cases
soft-brush pens
rotating lipstick mechanisms

When we were kids
we all wanted access to the heated upstairs bathroom
knock, knock, knock
"Just a minute girls I'm putting on my face"
Mum *never* went out without her "face"
not even to answer the door for the Jehovah's Witnesses

Now when I go see Mum
I like to doll her up
beads to match her blouse, earrings to match the beads
"It's hard putting someone else's lobe into an earring," Mum notes
as the floppy lobe evades her antique screw-ons
A bracelet of her choice
that bit of lipstick, garnet

"It's like playing dolls"
I happily reclaim

In the communal dining room
she reaps the praise
Frances! You look soooo nice!

There's nothing slow about me!

Made Young Again

For Eleanor Belyea Wees & Frances Firth Gammon,
founding poets of *The Fiddlehead*

Young poets
Frances and Eleanor
There they are, sitting on the Green
discussing heady ideas, tropes and rhymes
that might appear in the next *Fiddlehead*

Under the gaze of Bobby Burns
fountain pens jot lines, they
look at one another and smile
"This one," says Eleanor
holding aloft a poem
"I'll submit to the next meeting
of the Bliss Carman Society"
"I've got one ready too"
Frances displays her own
"I'm calling it 'Rain'"
They smile again because on this first warm day
of spring, the sun shines strongly

It is 1945
war not over yet
One has lost a first beau
The other will marry, move to Ottawa
Away, away as Thoreau said
Careers and children intervene
but they will write
diaries, letters, poems
inspire one another
stay in touch and touch one another
as time and distance
keep them from sitting together
on a bench on the Green

It is summer decades later
there are two young women sitting on the Green
discussing, gesticulating, clearly friends
one in a bright red jacket
one in a turquoise blouse
Their smiles are warm
their thoughts are long
words and ideas, joy flows between them
as they sit and talk
under the statue of Bobby Burns

I wander by
to catch a moment of their meeting
Why! It's Frances and Eleanor!

By the mere fact of coming together
made young again

You look young without trying.

Two Old Vets

Pauline and Frances
war year grads of 1943
University of New Brunswick

Pauline served in the Women's Auxiliary Air Force
Frances received love notes from the front
then lost George flying for Canada

Pauline remained unmarried—
though the feminist in me
rebels at the need to say that
Frances married a fellow poet
Her first two children raised on Brunswick Street
in Pauline's ramshackle Victorian home

Pauline, tough, eccentric
travelled the world alone, five continents
rode camels at the pyramids
Canoed, swam, sport her life's elixir
Her determination legendary
When arthritis disabled her
Pauline crawled from her car
to Killarney Lake to swim!

Pauline cherished animals
cats her lifelong companions
Thirty-two raccoons fed at her back stoop
I don't know what she thought of the boa constrictor
Frances kept when the son moved out and left it
Or the rats bred to feed the snake
but I am sure they exchanged wry looks

Pauline's New Year's parties
A must-do event, generations of alternative Fredericton society
gathering in the warm chaos of her Lincoln home
enjoying wassail and fruitcake from a century-old recipe

For years Pauline was the life of the community kitchen
delivered Meals on Wheels
When my father died Pauline came once a week
tending to her old friend Fran though she herself was old

I was there one Wednesday
Pauline's driving skills as extraordinary as she was
Within two city blocks she drove backward
down one-way Queen Street
knocked over a bicycle (without driver)
bumped a parking meter (without damage)
but we made it to the School Days Museum
Both former teachers, a perfect outing

Now Pauline and Frances are in homes
Homes for the elderly offer bingo, arts and crafts
church services, country music and *The Golden Girls*
maybe even a biannual trip to the mall
None of these homes have the simple agenda item
"Bring old friends together"
The homes keep them healthy, alive and apart

But Pauline and Fran have loved ones who understand
that old friends, old companions
might like to set eyes on one another
like young people do
The one wheelchair bus in Fredericton
burned out, was not replaced
So Carla and I go the extra mile
lift Frances physically from wheelchair to car
drive to Pauline's mountainless Mountain View Lodge

They've not met in over a year
Frances broke an arm, Pauline a hip
Both have memory loss
Cannot plan or anticipate a visit
It is going to be a surprise…
Precious, so precious

the recognition on their faces
in the cozy winter living room of Pauline's care home

"Pauline!"   "Frances!"

 I hand Pauline a piece of fruitcake
"Homemade… my father's recipe"
 Pauline takes a critical bite
"I know that cake, it's my mother's recipe"
"Yes, it is!" Frances agrees
"Pauline's mother gave it to Don
 when we lived on Brunswick Street"

 A deer passes by the big bay window
 I bang away at the parlour piano
 Two old vets savour fruitcake, hum along

You won't have anything to do when I'm in heaven.

"The Grave Is Not the Goal"

Frances and Kay
Campbellton girls
friends ninety years
though Fran was really friends first
with Kay's older sister Dorothy

"What happened to Dorothy, Kay?"
"Dorothy died"
"How did she die?"
"A stroke, a stroke carried her off"
"When was that?"
Kay does not know anymore

Kay and Frances cycled together
bike trips into their eighties
Fifty K a day, staying at B&Bs along the way
When asked by local newspapers
the secret of their aging success
they told of enjoying a nip of sherry
fooling a customs officer in Maine
when asked if they had alcohol
"Do you think little old ladies
would have such stuff?"
North shore of New Brunswick. Gaspé coast
Frances moved into her first home
with her "Emerald Queen,"
her forest-green mountain bike

Sometimes they cycled with Walter
"What happened to Walter, Frances?"
"Is he dead, Kay?"
"I don't know, did Walter die?"
"Bub Brebner. We were good friends.
He lived across the street."

Kay and Frances
skied downhill, cross-country
Kay carrying her beloved Scottie
on her chest in a baby pouch
They skied Grand Lake
Odell Park, Crabbe Mountain
athletic golden years
I remember when Mum saw snow and said
"If I can't ski anymore, what good is winter?"

"How old is your cat, Kay?
"Well," says Kay
  manoeuvring down from her fancy La-Z-Boy
"Lucy has a birth certificate"
  Still nimble despite arthritis
  Kay hops up, inspects a paper on the wall
"It says Lucy was born in 1994…
  what year is it now?"
Frances doesn't know
  I hesitate to interrupt the timelessness
"Lucy is seventeen," I say

"You're lucky to have your cat with you"
  Frances muses wistfully
"Oh, I wouldn't want to live without my Lucy."
"How old is she, Kay?"
"Well," says Kay, tipping down from her La-Z-Boy
"Lucy has a birth certificate"
  Again Kay goes to the wall
  again neither knows the year

Kay was a nurse, community health worker
caring for others a lifelong endeavour
A pet lover, an athlete
Frances an academic
historian, archivist

mother of four
They have been friends
since time immemorial

What happened to Dorothy? Walter?
How old is Lucy?
The conversation has a circular flair

Until Kay says "Life is real, life is earnest…"
and these two women who can no longer ski
bike, read a novel or remember the date
together recite verse after verse of Longfellow:

Life is real! Life is earnest!
And the grave is not the goal;
Dust thou art, to dust returnest,
Was not spoken of the soul.
…
Lives of great men all remind us
We can make our lives sublime
And, departing, leave behind us
Footprints on the sands of time.

—Henry Wadsworth Longfellow, "A Psalm of Life" (1838)

Among all of us we can get a complete memory.

"I Want to Die"

Frances, Betty and Don
from rural New Brunswick
log booms and pulp mills
mackerel and pickerel
hayfields and poverty
they made their way
to the city, the capital
"up the hill" to UNB
bobby socks and horn-rimmed glasses
shy, smart and loving words
met at a poetry club
the Bliss Carman Society

Betty and Don
Beaverbrook scholars
Don, a gay blade
with a tongue as sharp as a razor
Betty, mild and mannered as Clark Kent
brilliant and bluntly honest
Despite Don's reputation
for slicing people up with wit and criticism
he was always polite
always cordial to Betty

Why did Don give Betty those earrings
while sitting on the Green?
Did he not know this gift of adornment
would woo a lonely heart?

With Fran and Don it was mercurial
Visits to the Sun Grill
punctuated with pertinent debate
feuds and admonitions
(though Fran was with Dusty, *not* Don)
What was Frances thinking?

She had her James Dean look-alike
her work at the archives

And Don? Genteel to the ladies
glancing sidelong to the men
Enamoured with this older woman archivist

Did Frances want Don like Betty did?
What of this obtuse triangle?
All we know is, after years of saying no
Fran acquiesced and married the persistent Don
Shortly thereafter Betty walked into a lake
and floated instead of drowned

*

Betty moved in across the street
from Frances, Don, four children
The poet of University Avenue
who upon occasion needed a light bulb changed
by one of the Gammon boys
Was often to supper
proffered a signed book each Christmas

Decades fell like dominoes
Betty moved on, away from her proxy family
became renowned in those important literary circles;
twenty-three books and a professor emeritus later...
Don died

Betty, though almost blind
makes her last trip to Fredericton
to console Frances
Good old friends
to the end

As Frances' memory falters Betty's does not
She writes and calls, sends signed books less frequently

Until a stroke catapults Betty into a home and life of struggle

Now it is Frances' turn with daughter's help
to call and keep the contact
follow the painful recovery
"I can swallow again, walk with a walker"
Betty's voice less garbled each call
She's doing well, salvaged her spirit
"I listen to audiobooks, am dictating poems"

It's winter
helpful daughter makes the call out west
A nurse puts Betty on the phone
Her voice like rocks tossed in a blender
almost impossible to understand
She yells at Frances
"I want to die!"

"Where are you Betty?"
Frances is perplexed, unable to duly respond
I take the phone, try to console
say that Frances too was down
but now is doing well again

The call is over
I'm left to wonder
Is Betty depressed? Nearly gone?
Does she say that to everyone?

Or did she say at last to her dear old friend
what she wanted to say for sixty years
when Fran and Don were wed:
"I want to die"

Do I know that Betty is dead?

Ollie

The Sharpes lived across the street in Campbellton
Six children. Six children!
For an only child, a miracle of playmates
"I was always at the Sharpes'
Mrs. E. Sharpe taught music
she had a good name for it
Mr. Sharpe was a travelling tobacco salesman
Home on weekends: everyone towed the line"

Mum remembers all the Sharpes
"The two oldest were Bill and Donald,
then came Edith, Elsie, Ollie and John
Ollie was two years younger
I always begged my mother to take her along"

Countless old photos there is little Ollie
playing dolls with little Fran, tea party for two
small face and bangs, not conspicuous
always room for Ollie

Whatever became of Ollie?
Did she go on in school? Marry? Have kids?
I hope to pierce Mum's memory with an arrow
"I guess she stayed at home and grew older"

"Is Ollie alive?" Mum often asks
I don't know

Until one day a caregiver says
"There's someone here on respite
knows your mother... Olivia Sharpe"

Ollie? Ollie is alive!
I run to the room and there she is
a small, old woman with flat white hair and bangs
sitting in a wheelchair

Ollie Sharpe?
"Yes, who is there?"
I can tell by the way she does not look at me
Ollie is blind
It's Frances Firth's daughter

"Frances Firth!!! Is she here?!"
We are both excited
I feel like a kid
carrying a worn treasure map for years
in my back pocket, it suddenly unfolds
leads to a treasure

I run to Mum's room
Ollie is here Mum! Ollie Sharpe!

"Here?!"
Mum is not sure where *here* is
what miracle has occurred
"Ollie is alive?"
Yes, Mum, she's in a room down the hall
Let's go see her!

Without giving Mum time to digest Ollie's resurrection
I wheel her along a near century of memory
"Ollie!" Mum repeats in wonderment
And then there they are, the two old friends
in a room together

I wheel them face to face
Ollie, I've brought Frances Firth to see you

"Frances is here?!" Ollie looks around helplessly
Ollie is blind, I tell Mum
"You're blind Ollie?" Mum's first words
to her childhood playmate after eighty years

"Is that you Frances?"
"How much do you see Ollie?"
"Oh, light and dark—some shapes"
  Can you see Frances' face?
"No," Ollie confirms

  Does she look like Ollie? I ask Mum
"Oh yes, that's Ollie!"
  But Ollie is not so sure
  Mum's voice has aged

  I talk of Campbellton
  how the Sharpes lived across the street
  Yes, Ollie remembers
  she would go with Frances and her family
  up the Restigouche
"Up the Island," Mum says
"where Dr. Lunam let us use his camp
  a week every summer."
  For a brief moment the two girls meet
  in the big canoe on the Restigouche
  They are fishing and catch a tiny one
  that Mrs. Firth kindly fries up

  But soon it is clear that Ollie is not quite sure
  who she is supposed to know
  As the conversation flags
  I talk more than they do

  Soon it's time to go
  It is always time to go in a nursing home

  Goodbye Ollie, I say
  You've had a nice visit with Frances Firth
"Frances Firth! Is she here?!"
  Yes, you've just had a visit with her
  I press Ollie's hand goodbye
  Five minutes later, Mum too has forgotten the visit

Back in Berlin I see on my wall
a photo I've always loved
Mum, her mother and father
in a big canoe "up the Island"
Now I finally know that little girl with straight hair
After all these years I've met her

Mum's best little childhood friend
Ollie

Why drop dead if you can live to be in your nineties?

Learning to Die

The elderly are given very little credit for learning to die

All the expressions for coming into this world
hardly have equivalents for leaving this world
Being born, being no longer?
Growing up, growing down?
Learning to walk, unlearning to walk?
Raising a child, lowering the elderly?

All the things my aging mother has learned
To walk on pavement as if on ice
live with strangers, call an institution "home"
have patience when the nurse forgets her on the barred toilet seat
accept a body forever failing
let go of things
houses, cars, credit cards, bank accounts
power of attorney

Adjusting mentally to endless surprises
"Is this my room!?"
"Is this the Beaverbrook?"
"Where are we Carolyn?"
Finding out again and again
her husband isn't alive
friends, loved ones have passed on

It's no mean feat to take with equanimity
that one cannot bike or ski anymore
cannot swim, walk without assistance
or even get up from a chair

It is not easy learning to die

Years ago I spoke of celebrating
my fiftieth birthday a few years hence
Here, at the cottage Mum with all my overseas friends!

"But I won't be here then," she said accusatorially
as if my fiftieth would not be worth celebrating at all…
She was jealous of a future in a world without her

But she made it!
Guest-of-honour at the Grand Lake party
Fifty lobster on the beach
There is Frances proudly holding
a rainbow flag with her daughter

Now Mum no longer says
"I won't be here then"
Among other skills she has learned to let go

She accepts a Frances-less future
even if I do not

I say to myself, Do not die until after Carolyn comes.

Just Being

Can't take hearing
About any more friends dying
Mary's breast cancer
metastasized to bones and organs
Carolin's brain cancer
After two operations
she's in a coma
Gitta had a lumpectomy
they took forty-two lymph nodes
Cancer, cancer, cancer
You hit fifty and it's everywhere

My boss goes crazy
accusing secretaries
of trying to be something
more than she is
I must mediate, dedicate
hours hours emails emails
placate the boss, support staff
Cell phone messages
anytime day or night
One must *always* be available

My partner my soulmate
running herself into the next crisis
bankrupting us with good deeds
giving endless energy and resources
a society that never stops needing too much

My son, wonderful sweet brainy kid
so unique it's hard to be social—
what plagues his special soul?
Loves YouTubing and kayaking
What will his future hold?

I look forward to summer vacation
sawflies and crickets
stones skipping on a dawn pink lake
Spending time with someone
not hell-bent on accomplishing something
I want to stand in the wind
rake leaves, gather twigs
Prepare fish chowder
Look at old albums
Hold my mother's hand
Answer her questions

just be
just be

I just want to get on well with you until the end of our days.

The Offer of a Heart

For my grandmother, Maybel Grace Troop Firth

Though three thousand miles apart, you and I took a trip together last night Mum. It was late in Fredericton, later in Berlin but time didn't matter because we were back a century.

The year was 1912. Your mother Maybel Troop was in Dauphin, Manitoba. A hard-working, conscientious seamstress. A Methodist, a milliner who could also sew dresses, knit babies' booties, do needlepoint. A woman with golden hands could work her away around the world. Family legend has it that she made it all the way to California. "Following the seasons" it was called: spring, summer, fall and winter hat fashions.

Maybel's thin black notebook begins *Aug. 28, 1912*. With a friend from back east, Margaret… "That would be Margaret Chute," you add from your end of the phone line. A *millinery opening* followed soon by *not enough work to keep us from being homesick*, so they take up dressmaking to make ends meet.

At first, there is nothing emotional in Grannie's diary. Just facts and dates, prayers to God to grant her strength for her trials. *Fitted Mrs. Free, sold a hat, took two dresses for Ida Wilkinson… found the day too short.*

Then bits of private life invade. Margaret has her *Freddy.* Use of his first name, very intimate. Freddy brings chocolates! An act akin to proposing marriage it seems. But Freddy calls for Margaret, not Maybel.

This trip we're on, Mum, does not require memory of your life. It is happening six years before you were born so for once our call is not about what you cannot recall but what we can imagine together with the help of Grannie's sparse words.

It is November 8, Maybel's thirtieth birthday and she is homesick. *Wished I was home fifty times.* But then a pound cake arrives from home, a party is held. The next day is *a good day in millinery so feel quite cheerful.*

As the season follows to winter there is no mention of the weather, though December in Dauphin has an average low of minus twenty. No mention of world news, though Europe is mobilizing for war.

I crouch over my night light with a magnifying glass trying to decipher my grandmother's loopy inaccurate fountain pen script. "She did not have good penmanship," you say when I hesitate over a scrawl. An understatement. We riddle together. What could Maybel mean?

Headaches plague her. She attends services, sometimes every day. She calls on the heavenly father. Oh how to decide what is best to do with regard to the next season. *Dear Lord help us to make a right choice.*

By December 19, 1912, Maybel and Margaret have earned over one hundred dollars! Christmas comes and goes, two hats are sold. On New Year's Eve *Margaret had a big box of chocolates. We celebrated by eating them.* On January 2 they have made up their minds. The next season they will head back east.

And then, and then, it happens. January 14, 1913—*Enjoyed a delightful sleigh drive with Mr. Hart. Elegant evening.*

Suddenly, Mum, our travel into the past has a romance, a mystery.

"Mother always kept a photo of Billy Hart." Ah ha! He has a first name... and a photo! What became of him? I ask. You don't know. It was before your time and which parents speak of former beaus?

It is getting later and later. The other elderly residents must be long asleep. I should be too but now I want to know: what happened to Billy Hart?

I scan through the fittings and finished dresses, the church services, the calls from Freddy. Oh my god, Mum! Listen to this!!! January 22—*Mr. Hart took me for a sleigh drive into the country, beautiful moon light night—a drive long to be remembered.*

It is getting racy!

Then work, work, work. There are more sleigh drives. February 4—*I enjoyed being with Mr. Hart.*

Something has to happen. The ladies are leaving soon for the East. February 9—*League and Hart afterwards—wonderful if he could meet the conditions and said it was possible.*

What conditions??? If what were possible?!?

There is only one more step from here. And there it is on February 11—*Hart gave us a box of chocolates.* It is serious!

But it is all so last minute. Only a day after the chocolates Maybel and Margaret are scheduled to leave for the East. That is when his given name appears in Maybel's diary. *Bill has gone further west.*

What happened to Billy Hart Mum? I try you again on your end of

94

the phone. I've found that your mind is not a one-way street; sometimes it opens up roads long blocked. But no, you seem not to know more than I.

So all we can do now is keep reading. There are not too many pages left.

Everyone is sorry to see Margaret and Maybel leave Dauphin. The trip today is a flight away. In 1913 it takes a month, working along the way, stopping to see friends, staying at the YWCA.

All the while Maybel is waiting. Waiting for a letter? Waiting for something. Waiting for Hart to *meet the conditions?* Waiting.

March 7, 1913, back in New Brunswick, Maybel and Margaret part ways in Moncton. *Sorry to leave Margaret after being with her six months through sunshine and shadow.*

Back where Maybel began her trip, Campbellton, New Brunswick, the snow is piled high. *Disappointed in not having any mail.* Maybel catches a bad cold but manages two church services. She begins working *at the shop* immediately.

The more the days pass without a sign from Billy Hart the more desperate Maybel becomes in her pleas to God. *Give me wisdom to think, act and live.*

March 14, 1913, it has been *a month since we left Fair Dauphin and the crowd saw us off.* March 15—*Saturday and no letters.*

This is as good as Agatha Christie, I comment to Mum, unable to put down Grannie's diary until we know something, anything. My back is cramped, my eyes are blurring over the loops and swirls…

At last, on March 18. *The offer of a heart. God help me to choose aright and for both our good.*

Two days later: *Again, my father, I ask thy guidance in this the most important of life's questions, not only mine but that of others.*

But what actually is going on? *Life seems dull and colourless in spite of the new joy that has come to me at last.*

The choice is plaguing Maybel. On March 23 she writes four letters, *among them, one of a serious nature to one who would be my beloved some day if I will.*

Again she waits for a letter. March 27, 1913, the shop has its opening day. *First opening day in Campbellton. Wonder if it will be the last?* Already, her mind and heart are elsewhere, somewhere between the east and the west of a large Canadian country.

Mum and I pause. We know this cannot have a happy end. Maybel did not marry Billy. Grannie did not become a Hart; we know that. But for a moment in time, we too are in suspense like Maybel, wondering, waiting.

The second opening day is very stormy. March 31—*With this ends one quarter of 1913. What will another quarter bring me?* April 1—*Hope anticipation will not be better than realization.* April 3—*Received nothing: Patience is a virtue. Possess it if you can.* April 4—*Still waiting…* April 5… *and likely to be. I'm afraid. Alas! Alas!*

God is called upon again and again. *Dear Heavenly Father, answer the prayer I prayed tonight if it be thy will.* April 8—*My heart is still burdened.*

April 10—*A very busy day. Letters from G.E.G. and S.D.T. No time for idle dreaming.*

No time for idle dreaming? No time for idle dreaming!? What happened here!? Did the letters urge caution? Did Billy Hart not meet the conditions?

More letters, from sisters and from Hart himself. Hard work, prayer meetings. April 23, 1913—the diary ends.

What happened to Billy Hart? Maybe the answer is there between the lines or in diaries unseen.

The photo shows Billy Hart in uniform. One in ten Canadian soldiers was killed in WWI. Google reveals many Canadian William Harts served. Some were killed; I send his photo to the archivists. But it is not known.

Maybe Maybel loved Mr. Hart in her *idle dreams* for years. Maybe it was only after hearing of his death in 1917 that she agreed to marry the widower Dougald Firth, thirty years her senior.

What happened to Billy Hart? We may never know. But in the hours it took to read the cryptic love affair of these hundred-year-old lovers, you and I Mum, we've been "strolling down nostalgia lane" as you put it, going on a sleigh drive in Dauphin, Manitoba, at minus twenty degrees on a moonlit night.

Mum would be 130?
Well, I guess I can't expect her to be home at that age.

What's Left of Her

At a hometown gallery opening
a well-meaning, good old friend of the family
says she visited my mother recently
"or I visited what's left of her"

I seethe inside
My beautiful, struggling mother

Yes, I can see logically
Mum's abilities have ebbed
She had to move out of her own home
stop biking, walking
Lost her precious reading and writing
Her mind "wanders"
She needs assistance

But let me tell you
good old friend
what is left of Frances

Mum has her vocabulary
a vast one, more than most
She can still spell and define
obscure words, even in Latin!
Her wit, sharp and strange
Sometimes every line a twist
a pun of the day
I call them "Francesisms"

The days have gone by and I'm still here

Why rush through life when you can go at a snail's pace?

Even her memory loss can be intriguing
"How old am I Carolyn?" Ninety-three Mum

"That's ridiculous—I didn't live that long!"
And she laughs

Mum enjoys life
In front of a campfire
expressions of pleasure
as rich as any Buddhist
A sunset she watches like a thrilling film

Maybe, old friend, you've not seen Frances
sipping tea from the pink lacy Limoges
her mother's best china
Add a date square, now *that's* an event!

Go through those thick black paper albums
Mum can identify fifteen girls at summer camp 1928
"That's Natalie, she had *beautiful* red hair!"

Take her outside—
not to unfamiliar streets near the nursing home—
but to the Green by the Saint John River
where chipmunks play hide-and-seek in the willow
Pour a cup of thermos tea
There she is 100 percent Frances!

Talk about *the cottage* and Mum's mind lights up
a firefly on a dark night
Magical Grand Lake
its eternal promise of summer
"Will I get there another year Carolyn?"
Where there's yearning there's something left

At the nursing home they ask us caregivers
to compile a list of songs loved ones enjoy
Students record them on iPods
Each resident can hear her favourite tunes
with the press of just one button

I buy a 1920s Canadian songbook
Mum knows half by heart
Nursery rhymes, poems by Wordsworth
all in her long-term hard drive

Of course it is difficult to see a dear old friend grow older
It's hard on me too, the daughter who so loves
what's left of her

But can't you just see Frances now?
Sitting in her room, watching the sunset
sipping tea from the Limoges
her earphones on, humming along
to her favourite old songs

Tell the prime minister that I am enjoying old age.

My Mother the Astronaut

Every call home I try to pull her back
Like a stray satellite
our gravity connection weaker

I use all the right words
family words, familiar words
but sometimes she cannot relate to
Don her late husband
home wherever that could be
after a lifetime of homes

We agree that as long as we know
you are my mother
I am your daughter
we are doing well

Pull, pull, gently tug
I am doing this memory work
not only for Mum
I need to hear her voice
mother dopamine

Tonight when I called the nurse said
"Good thing you called, your mother wants to go home"
I *am* her home, I say
I am my mother's memory home

Every call I recreate her world
"Remember Mum" a game we play
Remember Mum
we used to play badminton in the yard beside the house
"Oh yes!" she is excited to share a memory
"By the tennis courts!"
I start pulling

What tennis courts Mum?
"By the old house up a little winding path"
I catch on, it is *her* childhood home

Sometimes I pull her back
sometimes I let her drift
an astronaut on an ever-lengthening cord
She is my mother
but I have become the mother station

"When are you coming home Carolyn?"
A question I dislike
a day or two after an overseas visit
that she has already forgotten
A question I like
when I am planning the next trip
A question I love when I can say
Soon Mum!
In four weeks, three, two, one
Countdown!
Our orbits about to intersect
"A week! Oh! That is wonderful!"

By the end of an hour
My mother is back
sharing references
"I love this photo with the four sails
It's Geoff's isn't it?"
She named my brother
knew it was his work

"I'm in my room," she says

I've done it
Once again
I've brought her home

Each call, each visit
I hold you in my orbit Mum
With every bit of cosmic strength

I will not stop until you are stardust

You renew my memory.

Super Fran

Maybe ten times in ten years
Frances donned a cape
became "Super Fran"
chatty all-knowing
omniscient narrator of her own life

I'd love a scientific explanation
A woman who could not name one resident
suddenly names eighteen
Could not say if she'd had lunch
lists dinner ingredients down to the missing mayonnaise
Could not remember her daughter-in-law's name
asks after Renée and the three children
Who for months had not said "yesterday"
recounts events from days before

I learned *never* assume
my mother couldn't remember
Realized she took it all in
stored it... somewhere
with once-in-a-while access

Sometimes after a trauma
a dear friend dying
seeing her old house empty
finding me gone
Her mind jumpstarted
a frenetic scramble
for what was thought lost

These were exciting times
I alerted siblings
Call Mum! She remembers!

Not only remembers
analyzes, puzzles things through
As if the sphinx that guarded the gates of her mind
gave away riddles

It sounded something like this:

We had a little snowstorm yesterday
When I woke this morning I was so dismayed
because you weren't here
It wasn't my room
It was so empty
They told me: It can't be high tension all the time

I woke with this dreadful pain in my back!
Pressed this thing on the bed three times
I fell out of bed, put on a great show
Everyone thought I should have a cigarette and a drink
I am getting to be a loose lady
After I took Gravol I felt better

I said to Don tonight I just loathe smoking
One never knows when one might smoke and fail
Don used to smoke heavily
never lost the longing

My father apparently smoked as a young man
Did you know he took a course in business at McGill?
That was where he met Mr. Dawson
head of Canadian Cottons
who suffocated on the train
Eleanor kept up better correspondence with Betty
I was astounded that Betty died
I guess she was quite blind
Ollie is dead
I believe she was blind too

I had a lovely long card from Leona
She half writes half prints
She was on a big trip with her believers in New Zealand
Something-of-the-Redeemer

Today we had a meeting with Sandra
We looked at photo albums
Sandra said, "My, your mother was handsome"
That's the best compliment Mother ever had!
In one photo Dorothy is screwing up her face
because she didn't like having her photo taken

Dr. Bailey had a granddaddy look
Dr. Downey sent photos of his grandchildren
He gave me something to relieve the pain

That's the third or fourth time Paula and Sandra visited
They're so good about coming
I have to try to be merry

There's a nice fish pond here
I play with the fish
I talk to them and think
they have such a nice life
There are Redeemers in the fish pond

There was one woman today who was very fond of cats
She brought this pretty orange one
You know the table where you and I sat?
There was movement under it
The cat had gotten under the tablecloth!

I woke up so dazed
I read the thing you put on the board
"Remember you're in your own room"

I am out in the hall
My tea is there but no toast
You top it all off by calling!

Now... we all know Don is dead
and there may not be Redeemers in the aquarium
but my mother sent me Googling
A.O. Dawson, head of Canadian Cottons
did indeed die in his berth on a train
en route to Toronto, January 10, 1940

*Grade 1 Miss Doak; Grade 2 Miss Dickie; Grade 3 Miss
Andrew; Grade 4 Miss Crocket; Grade 5 Miss Baird; Grade 8
Mr. Jameson and Mr. Delong; Grade 9 Miss McNaughton;
Grade 10 Miss Quinn. She had buns of red hair; she never
married. She was very impatient with the kids who didn't
do well but great for those of us who did.*

Leftover Family

"It's a good thing you called!"
 Why Mum, what's up?
"Well, mother is gone now
 I'm very lonely
 We are the leftover family
 You should come home
 We can live together
 I'll try to get work
 as a maid if need be"

This conversation might have made a smidgeon of sense
decades ago when Mum's mum died
when I didn't live in Germany with my own family
If Mum weren't living in a care home

In Mum's tumble of words I hear
churn, churn, churn
Grey matter crunching
How did she end up
in a home she does not know
Generations dead
family split
Something has to be done
It's urgent

Even in the safety of a home for the elderly
the mind is not safe

We are the leftover family

I have three siblings
but at this moment, not in Mum's mind
I am the only one she has plans for

My mother was an enabler
could make things happen

So, lying in her bed at night
she has to work it out
"We have to make our family dividends pay
Maybe Jennifer could join us, help with expenses"
At least my sister is alive again

I assure her all costs are covered
She is suspicious
"Really? With what money!?"
Your pension, Don's, savings
You're fine Mum, everything's covered

"But can you live…"
she hesitates "…with Don?"
The estrangement from my father
haunts Mum a decade after his death

I know how to distract her
lead her into less shark-infested waters
Tell her I've joined a choir, sing to her
weave non-sequiturs back into her tapestry of life
Like a bard I recreate her village
right there on the phone
until she's forgotten
we need to work things out

Memory loss is good for forgetting your worries
though some little thing is still niggling
"How did you find me here?"
Your number hasn't changed
455-3138 always the same
"Oh, I took it with me"
Yes, you can do that now
"And where am I?"

The whorl recreates itself
Off we go again

Mum and I weave, spiral
the ultimate conversation of now

Over an hour later
I say I'll call again
"That's nice, I'll go to sleep tonight
knowing you can get a hold of me"

Wouldn't it be great if just by a prick of a finger
we could be transported... you to me and me to you?

Between Heartbeats

I am online when the email arrives
The RN thinks to start with the line
"Your mother is fine"

Another resident found her
lying sideways on the floor
still in her wheelchair
No visible injury, no pain
no recollection how it happened
that it happened

The emails come sporadically
Some don't start with the line she's fine
"Your mother was found
lying on the bathroom floor
in the hall, between chairs…"

At the end of these endless scenarios
they remember to assure me
She can move limbs normally
she's back in bed

I don't tell my siblings
Why should more than one of us worry?
There's nothing any of us can do
and after all, Mum's fine

But maybe I should tell them

Let them know about that moment of dread
before I see the word *fine*
Let them know
between emails
my heart beats with my mother's

Which is harder, babyhood or old age?

Zen

Even if my three flights
last twenty-four hours
I have to see her that eve

Arriving breathless with anticipation
eager to embrace my dear Mum

This time she was in the rec room
a barbershop quartet
entertaining the guests

"Old Songs Are Just Like Old Friends"
the foursome complete the chord in soothing harmony

I sit beside her
Mum turns and says
"Just wait 'til this is over Carolyn"

Time collapses
a string with two ends brought together
I just stepped out of the room
a visit ago
now I am back

We listen together tapping toes
then she turns to me and smiles

My Buddhist brother says
Mum has learned the first lesson of Zen:
living in the now

The nearer you get to forever the better.

Does She Know You?

The first thing most people say
when I tell them my mother has memory loss
is not I'm sorry for that, or
How's her health? Is she happy?
but the knee-jerk reaction:
"Does she know you?"

This has happened so many times
I am beginning to think it's a conspiracy
What do they *really* mean?

Ideally they mean Oh, how hard for you
How sad to lose the mother-daughter-ness

But I'm afraid what's really behind
that automatic question is something different
Something that implies
If she doesn't know you, it's all over
If she doesn't know you, why bother?
If she doesn't know you, give up

A shopping mall chance encounter
there's that question again
I don't have time to say
Well, yes, she usually knows me
but sometimes she talks about me in the third person
Hears my voice on the phone, tells me Carolyn called
Looks at my photo and names me to me
Sometimes, no—she doesn't know me
Not for that moment
I have to remind her: Mum—it's me, Carolyn
"You're Carolyn?" She looks around for me
where I was a moment before
Then I trip on her outstretched foot
"Sorry Carolyn!"

But in the Regent Mall, fluorescent lights glaring
bags hanging heavy on our arms
no one really wants to hear all that
They want to know
Venetian blinds yes, no, yes, no
She-knows-you-she-knows-you-not

Yes might mean
Oh, perhaps I should get in touch with Frances
drop her a note, drop by even
No might mean
Well, if she doesn't know you, her daughter
she certainly won't know me
so it's no use visiting

There by Atlantic Lotto
where you can buy a chance on the future
I want to give a lecture on dementia
How it's not either/or, not a cul-de-sac
there are alleys, hidden pathways
That people with memory loss
still know the beauty of colourful gerberas mixed with roses
still know a wrapped gift is yearning to be opened

I want to tell them, Go see Mum! Try her out!
Sometimes something she's not expressed
her entire lifetime springs out of her
Like a high diver off a board
she executes a perfect mental moment
something new, unique like
"The past seems more solid than the future"

All a bit much for my mall encounter
so I usually just say "Yes, she knows me"

I've seen the difference between yes and no
A woman who is visited every day
by her son at the York Care Centre says to me

"This lovely man says he's my son"
I see the love and care and time
this loving son brings and how that love
is part of him

And this is what I really want to say
to everyone who asks "Does she know you?"

Why do you ask?
I know her

I say to my stuffed animals, "Is it still me?"
And they all nod their little heads

Ramps

Why would one expect
blind people to read the printed page
deaf people to hear a sigh
those with memory loss
to find their way back from the bathroom?

Ramps are built
for people in wheelchairs
What of ramps for the mind?

In Mum's room
I install our childhood blackboard
During visits a simple note
See you after lunch, love Carolyn
Mum is not exactly sure when that is, "after lunch"
but it lets her know I'm in town
comfort message

If we see an old friend
I meet Mum's memory at the pass
"Mum! It's Marg!"

In conversation I replace pronouns with names
say Jennifer each time
so she knows throughout
it's about Jennifer

Her favourite son-in-law does crosswords
by phone west to east coast
prompting Mum with clues
until she solves the words alone

She creates her own ramps
asks rather than states
"Was I ever here?"
Speaks with salt-and-pepper doubt

"This doesn't look too familiar"
Hones handy phrases
"My mind plays tricks on me"

An old acquaintance
might converse with Fran
never know her memory
is like Swiss cheese
I provide ramps my heart needs
Hey Mum! I'm calling so you can wish me a happy birthday!
Hey Mum! See those flowers in your room, they're from me
Happy Mother's Day!

In twenty years
I may want help too
At the airport
a check box that says
"Memory loss—please assist"

A ramp to help me home

If I can't remember your name
I'll just call you "daughter without a name"
until you tell me what it is.

In My Mother's Words

"We should be brave and stay sensible to the very end
I think I slip every day
I don't think men slip as much as women

I thought you were married"
Yes, I married a woman
"That's a pretty big slip
We are just two slippers

I am as crazy as Moondog
I don't like my old friends to see me like this, since I've slipped
I'll slip so far I won't know who I am

I dreamt all night long and woke up crazy
I always predicted I'd go mental
I used to have little spells of being crazy when I was younger
thought it was a sign of my mind giving out
It wasn't a very nice feeling, I felt I was going"
Well, you haven't gone very far
"No, but I wanted to

I thought my mother went a little odd
I tried to talk to her as often as I could to keep her sane
I put paint on her nails
She said, 'Don't put paint on my nails—
it will look as if I know what I'm doing, and I don't'

What are we doing down at the cottage this time of year?"
It's summer
"I can't enjoy myself as I used to
I hope this doesn't happen to any of you people
Do you show signs of going mental?"
A bit
"That's too bad
You were so good in school

You were always so good to everyone
I admired you"
Give yourself a break Mum, you're ninety-six
"No! I really went mental
O dear Lord, please help me to be sensible again
I don't want to go out of my mind even if I am an old lady
Help me not go totally insane

Poor Kathi, having to have relatives like me
She said, 'You're not crazy Frances. You just think you are'
I said, 'If you think you're crazy, you are crazy'
You can put me in the asylum in Saint John
They know what a crazy person is—
she does silly things like talking to herself all the time

I think I'll go for a naked swim
Do you think that would scare the populace?
Now that everyone thinks I'm crazy, I can show them

When I went through my crazy stage
no one paid any attention to me
I turned crazy and stayed that way"

How do you define crazy?
"I gave up trying to be sensible—very bad feeling"
You don't find it comfy to let your mind drift a bit?
"No, I don't, I think it's being thoughtless
You act silly and your family puts you in an asylum
I went in there with my fingernails painted
They said, 'Look, she's started to paint her fingers—that's a sign...'
I am getting itchy behind my ears... that's a sign
Even the big toe on my right foot is acting up again
That's a sure sign

I never thought you acted crazy Carolyn"
Thank you Mum
"I thought, of all my children, you were the most sensible"

I don't know if that's true…
Anyway, I don't think you're going crazy Mum
"Thank you very much"

Katharina pokes her head into the room:
There'll be a nice crackling fire when you get up
"She made a nice crackling fire for us
We better get up and enjoy it
I felt my mind was totally gone
But I certainly could enjoy a nice crackling fire"

You can be thankful if you stay sane through life.

A Day in the Life of a Bug-in-a-Rug

A big day
Paula has moved to new digs
My mother's friend from Normal School 1937
We are invited to lunch

Faithful Paula visits Mum weekly
her walker in the taxi trunk
navigates the long corridors
to Mum's room and memories

Today it's time to visit Paula
but Mum is… droopy
exhausted, narcoleptic
eyes impossibly glued shut
Not the first time, I know the score
urge her to move with military commands
In return, a litany of epithets
"Why am I going out? No one wants to see me
I have no teeth, I'm of no use to anyone
Why are you dragging me out in this condition?"

All this interspersed with fitness-studio up and at 'ems
Paula is such a good friend, you have lots of teeth
You can rest right after, your cousin Mary is 103

"Is she still alive?"
Humour gives me hope

It's a battle of the wills
Mum, to stop the show
versus my life-is-good-at-all-costs

One more rant from Mum
"I'm so lonely, my family has all left me
Life is not worth living, take me home"

As I search for Mum's hand, up her sweater sleeve
I stop midway, almost leave Paula
waiting expectantly at the door of her new home
Mum feels me succumb
In our yo-yo symbiosis, she now takes the initiative
inaudibly, a sigh "Well, okay then"

We manage somehow
Mum barely makes the transfers, leaning on me
as if her legs are mud

"Open your eyes Mum. LOOK!"
Frances sees Paula, smiles wanly
Paula is very happy to see us
proudly shows us her new dining room

The attendant looks somewhat askance
as I organize my mother with mandates
"Pick up your spoon! Look at the soup!"
Paula is unfazed
She has roused Mum herself many a time

Lunch is over, soup half eaten
we go to see Paula's new room
Lovely! Isn't it lovely Mum!?
No response
Wow, your own kitchenette!
a walk-in shower… wow, wow!

After a bit I leave the two old friends
together alone
If I stay, I will do all the talking

Soon get a call
"Your mother's back is sore
She wants to go home and rest"

That's that
Mum rallies to wave like a solar queen
wrist flick back and forth
Paula says how good it's been to see Frances

I feel like a torturer

It's four p.m. in Fredericton
bridge construction, traffic to a trickle
In a moment of inspiration, I say
Shall we wait out rush hour on the Green?
Mum nods

Fresh air, squirrels and flowers
blue river backdrop to billowing willows
with every minute Frances returns to life
They say the elderly sundown after four
but Frances sun ups
I push my luck
How 'bout a trip to the mall?
Oh yes! She chooses her own new pyjamas
red flannel with blue and pink bow ties
Undershirts, socks—what a day!
Supper at the food court, Tim Hortons chili
watch mallgoers as if at the Royal Ascot

Back in her room we call Newfoundland
Mum rises to her intellectual best for Peter her genius son
They discuss the geology of the Avalon Peninsula
engaged, witty, strong of voice

The helpers come to bathe Mum
She returns, her grey hair fluffed about her head like a halo
new red PJs soft and cuddly

"One of my aunts," she tells me
"used to call me her bug-in-a-rug

Whenever she'd see me she'd say
'How's my little bug-in-a-rug?'"

It's a rare new story

I help Mum into bed
negotiate a comfy nighttime position
write a note on the blackboard
See you tomorrow after lunch

Good night Mum
I kiss her forehead
Mum has clean sheets
snuggled up under her chin
She smiles and says contentedly
"I'm just a little bug-in-a-rug"

Life is so beautiful on a bed under a blanket. O, sweet rest.

Her Warble

I had to wait 'til my mother was over ninety
to hear her sing

She was one of those children
told to stand at the back and just move her lips
"Don't sing Frances!" and she didn't

As kids, we asked her to join in
but she told us she was tone deaf

Yet somewhere inside she must have hummed along
must have learned the words

Because now nearing one hundred she sings joyfully
golden-oldie tunes
"Shine on, shine on harvest mooooon…"
Punctuates each tick tock of "My Grandfather's Clock"
Knows every line of obscure Methodist hymns

You sing so much better now Mum!
She accepts the compliment with grace

In her home, which we both pretend is her home
we are now a familiar duet
known to sing all six verses of "Good King Wenceslas"
at the annual Christmas party

They say dementia steals the soul
diminishes, is such a shame
but I tell you
it has given my mother back
her warble

I didn't know my age. I'm glad you told me.

Fingerprint

Don't let anyone tell you
that your loved one
is like this or that

As my mother aged
so did her friends
The Campbellton Girls
legendary girl group
The Beatles of northern New Brunswick
They had fans
they had reunions
and they aged
each one differently

Pauline who lost mobility
kept her world intact by phone
her room in the home a UN switchboard
Edith who lost names
retained social graces
"It's lovely to have you here"
Kay who lost language
could still enjoy albums
point out the Campbellton Girls sepia 1931

Catch-all terms
Alzheimer's, dementia
do not catch all

We were told to call a spade a spade
"vascular dementia"
proper term, label it
but knew that word *dementia*
would give my mother grief
So in all those years
never said it in her presence

Recited faculties she possessed
eyesight, hearing, health and wit
It's natural to forget things
at such a biblical age
we all agreed

I know we were lucky
Mum aged politely, funny, sociable
New caregivers greeted me in awe
"You're Frances Gammon's daughter?!"
My mum the rock star

For those who feel dementia
is an on-off switch
a licence to forget the forgetful
let me tell you from the source
it is engrossing and difficult
exceptional and stirring
distressing and compelling

Unique as a fingerprint

If you are pushing me in a wheelchair,
people will think you're my daughter.

I Love You

Hackneyed, cliché
not of the older generation
against the Gammon rules
our family never said it

Even when it came in vogue
in every film, on every lip
coffee mugs, bumper stickers
still, we didn't say it

Too intimate, too much

Mum grew older
from far away over the phone
I began
I love you Mum

"Oh, you're such a nice daughter"
disconcerted I'd changed the rules

Age mellows
but Mum remained firm
though telling me in so many ways
she never said those words

Until one day
I think she was ninety-five
popping out of her
a magician's bright bouquet

No qualifiers
no need for me to say it first
For one moment
the Gammon taboo
forgotten

"I love you Carolyn"

Call again and if I'm not on this earth
I'll lean down from heaven and give you a little hug.

The Fiddlehead

Some things, you never forgot

Your name and mine
The cottage, summer incarnate
Ganong Chicken Bones—sticky pink cinnamon chocolates
The pattern of your mother's china

And *The Fiddlehead*
thin collection of mimeographed poems
breathed into life in a small city of eastern Canada
as the last of sixty million died in WWII
The war that took your childhood sweetheart
The war that mocked poetry
Soon *The Fiddlehead* poets
would be questioning the human soul
with words like Nagasaki

You strove to express the inexpressible
Fellow poets became lifelong friends
the first editor, your husband
But the fifties put women in the home
Suddenly only Don had founded *The Fiddlehead*
Between migraines and turkey dinners for seven
no room for a mother-who-had-been-a-poet

Decades cascaded
and the name of this magazine
became a pilot-light to your literary self
The Fiddlehead brought a wishful gleam to your eye
years you called the best of your life

A cherished photo of you
reading one of your *Fiddlehead* poems
two homecare workers listening lovingly

Our Frances
the poet

I haven't done much poetry writing since I turned a Gammon.

On Her Own Terms

Let's be kind
call the people who were ready
to see my mother die
before she was ready
"Angels of Death"

The first one, a decade before Mum died
decided a bad back needed killer doses of morphine
The Angel of Death was shocked
when daughters called outside authorities
Morphine was stopped
After three weeks in bed Mum walked down the hall
"I thought she was a ghost," a caregiver said

Some years later Mum broke an arm
My brother arrives at hospital to an empty cot
In Emergency an Angel decided there was no room for her
My ninety-four-year-old mother with memory loss
(and let's not forget, a broken arm)
bumps over two hours of New Brunswick winter roads
upriver to the next hospital
Family not informed

I never heard her so grim
I think she thought she would die there
with no one around

My mother's next encounter with an Angel of Death
came during a flu epidemic
Three residents had already died
Mum could no longer swallow
I was called in Berlin
If I wanted to see her one last time…

My sister and I debated if in her weakened state
it made sense to send Mum to hospital

A caregiver at the home, an Angel of Life it turned out
said revolutionary words "Ask your mother"

A nurse cradles the phone to her ear
Mum, do you want to go to hospital for intravenous?
In this life and death situation
Mum's mind as bright as a starry sky
Her swollen voice weak but clear
"Yes, that would be nice"
Are you sure Mum? It can be chaotic there
I ask three different ways, three times
Yes, yes, yes.

The Angel of Life warns
"Send an advocate with her, if not
they'll just fill her with morphine and send her back"
Thanks for the warning!
A call to my brother: Go with her, be her advocate
She is admitted to palliative
Geoff sends a photo *Hydrating with bunny*
I burst into tears
The photo sustains me three flights and twenty hours

There's Mum!
life-saving liquids running into her arm
Emerges from a fog to make a request
I've never heard before
"Can I put my arms around you?"
She grasps me like a long-lost teddy

The next morn quick coffee before heading to hospital
Doctor calls "Your mother is being discharged now"
Oh! I am surprised, is she swallowing?
"No"
Do you know why?
"No"
You are sending her back... to die?!
Silence

I have flown from overseas,
 give me a day or two with my mother!
"She has been here a week
 You are prolonging her death"
WHAT!?!?
My mother has been in hospital for a day!
I hear a chart being checked... Oh... yes... hmmm
Angel of Death flaps wings backward
allows me time with my mother
That afternoon Mum clears the cement in her throat
and is fine

By chance that eve
 they serve Mum's favourite puréed chowder
 salty, fishy, warm
"This is so good!"
 She eats it to the last spoonful

They are overjoyed to see her at the home
"So few return," I'm told
 Mum hams it up
 clasped hands raised over her head
 like a boxing champion

This summer at the cottage
Mum waved the New Brunswick flag
in the warm easterlies of Palmer's Point
as if to say I'm here... I'm still here
She takes relish in snipping strawberries for shortcake

How many Angels of Death did my mother survive?
None of them bad people
None of them mean
Well-intentioned angels making way for the younger and fitter
deciding for the elderly it's time to die

But when my mother did go it was her own doing
no broken bones, no illness, no drugs

Slowly she stopped eating, stopped drinking
I received that final call in Berlin
Mum waited for me

No Angel of Death hovered over her
I asked if she wanted to go to hospital
"No" she was fine and comfy she said
Still speaking, still smiling
still giving me love
letting me know
Carolyn—it's time
on her own terms

Do you think we'll see each other again before we die?
Whoops! That was a slip of the tongue!

Epilogue

I remember the first time my mother did not know who I was. I had taken her on a trip to the Annapolis Valley of Nova Scotia where her mother came from and where my mother spent childhood summer holidays. Maybe the past impinged too much on the present and set her back in time. We woke in our shared B&B room and she said, "Who are you?"

"Mum, it's me, Carolyn..."

"You're not Carolyn!"

I learned to take these blank-outs with good humour. "Well, I am calling you Mum, so you must be my mother." But her memory loss was not monolithic. It was patchy like a worn woven carpet; from different angles she knew different things at different times.

My mother *always* knew that she was not at home, even when the term "home" shifted in her mind to various homes she had lived in. We found an adage for her situation: It's not *where* you live, it is what you do with your life where you live. Over the years of her memory problems, she lived in three different places and for prolonged stays at the hospital. When she moved to a full-care facility she had to leave familiar items behind yet again. It struck me that we often ask our elderly to master new social and emotional situations that would be strenuous for people decades younger.

Like most of us, my mother wanted to live a good long life. And she wanted to determine what a good life was, not have someone else tell her if her life was worth living or not. Despite the failure of the system at times to protect her right to live, she did, in the end, live a good long life. There were ups and downs and learning curves, moments of frustration and jubilation. One big thing I learned in the last fifteen years of my mother's life is that it is not all downhill for the elderly. My mother had a phase of doing "poorly" (as she put it) when she was ninety-three, but then an excellent year when she was ninety-four. I learned never to say never. I learned to cherish what she was able to do and not focus on what she couldn't.

About one-third of us will face some type of memory loss as we age. We must not abandon them, or ourselves! What are the guidelines? The helpmates? I am hoping that by documenting this part of my mother's life in poems I can help others creatively cope and know that memory loss is not an insurmountable barrier to living a good life.

The journey for both of us was full of surprises and each one became a poem. I thought I would publish them soon after her death, but some years have gone by. I realized I was hesitating to put them into the public realm because I wondered—would Mum have wanted me to? Frances Firth Gammon was such a woman of her times. She was the first in her family to attend university. She was fashionable and smart. She was a published poet and founding member of Canada's oldest literary magazine, *The Fiddlehead*. She was one of the first female assistant professors at the University of New Brunswick and the university's first archivist. On top of an MA in history she took a degree to become a librarian. She married late in life and had four baby boomers into her forties. In 2002 a book of her early poetry was published: *There Was the Lord Adjusting His Binoculars*. It didn't seem fair after such an accomplished life for me to focus this book on the latter years. Yet I know now that this too is one of her life's accomplishments: how she lived those last years with much of the fortitude and creativity that had made her earlier years so fulfilling.

Mum had been an avid correspondent, her letters erudite and full of friendly advice. As she lost the ability to write it occurred to me that maybe she could still dictate letters. In this way, we continued her correspondence years longer. This led to me recording my mother's pithy original quips, the Francesisms. Some of them seemed born of her changing mind they were so otherworldly. She came up with so many of them I filled pages and pages and they ended up being a spotlight on her intellectual self, still there, still shining but in a different form. My mother's memory loss was not her; it was part of her.

To complete this book, I decided to make the Francesisms an integral part of it, to have her "comment" on my efforts to record her life. My mother loved learning, going to university, any intellectual pursuit. Her memory loss interfered with that but did not bring her thoughts to a halt, as anyone who had close contact with her in the last years will testify. In this collection of poems I have tried to document her struggles but also the achievements of living with memory loss.

I'd hate to go to the next world without being quoted.

Acknowledgements

A West African proverb says: "It takes a village to raise a child." I would like to paraphrase by saying: "It takes a village to help an elderly person live in comfort and dignity and with joy in life." I would like to thank the community members of the village who allowed me and my mother to enjoy her last decade on her own terms, which in turn made this book possible.

I would like to begin by saying to my life partner, Katharina Oguntoye: "Ich danke Dir tausendmal"—Thank you one thousand times! Thank you for saying "Yes—go and see your mother," for saying "Yes— fly, don't worry about the cost" or "Yes," you would look after our son Noel in my absence. Without this 100 percent partner support, I could never have spent the time I did commuting between Berlin, Germany, and Fredericton, New Brunswick, to be there for my mother. And thank you Noel for learning at a very young age to take the frailties of the very old with equanimity.

Next I would like to thank my mother's peers who, as her memory wavered, their commitment to her did not. Kay Carr knew my mother for over ninety years and until Kay could no longer do so herself, welcomed Frances like a sister each and every visit. Paula Ingersoll, just a year younger than Mum, never accepted "I don't remember" from her friend. "C'mon Frances, you do remember!" and then, Mum did. Pauline Cunningham came faithfully once a week after my father's death; she understood grief needs company. Companions from the University of New Brunswick Bliss Carman Society and *The Fiddlehead* magazine Elizabeth Brewster and Eleanor (Belyea) Wees provided Frances with intimate epistolary friendships highlighted with calls and annual visits. They connected my mother to her intellectual past and kept her humour wry and honest, as did Marjory and Allan Donaldson, artist and author, who never failed to entertain Frances with salmon and sherry in their private *salon*. Jacky Webster, a luminary in her own right who worked as a journalist into her nineties, kept me sane with fireside chats. Jacky and her daughter Allison Brewer were great friends to both me and my mother. This indomitable team of mostly nonagenarians grounded Mum in her generation and gave her a sense that she was still part of an intact social circle. Many of them have now passed but I want the people who enabled these friendships to know how much Frances and I appreciated your support.

Then there was "team Fredericton." Without my strong gang of friends in Fredericton I could never have done what I did. This team begins with my precious friends Tristis Ward and Dianna Murray, whose house I stayed in for over two decades. It wasn't always easy. I took four emergency flights home. One might imagine the state I was in each time. Thank you Tris and Di. Your generosity and compassion surpassed friendship; it was a loving kinship. When they could not host me, Carla Rasmussen and Tracey Rickards stepped in with gracious hospitality and, not to be forgotten, the cat-petting sessions that transported Frances to cat-heaven! And Carla, a huge thank-you for facilitating the visits with Pauline! Arlene Glenncross—thank you for your legal help over the years and Jackie Greenman for the massages! Thank you for all the wonderful invitations where Mum was an honoured guest. Maureen Toner, thank you for the drives in the countryside and the visits with Feisty and for never shying away from helping out when Mum was most vulnerable. Carmen Poulin and Lynn Gouliquer—what can I say—gourmet meals and warm flannel shirts on your terrace, superb! Susan O'Donnell, I will never forget the game of Scrabble when Mum was nearly gone on morphine. There are many more of you who always asked after my mother, included her in invitations or offered to lend a hand. Thank you from the bottom of my heart.

At the cottage at Grand Lake our neighbours were a constant source of generous friendship and goodwill—thank you to the Beltrandi and Panza-Gosa family. Also to Israel and Marlene Unger for the family-filled lakeside dinners and Izzy, thanks for daring to take a ninety-two-year-old out in a speedboat! A BIG thank you goes to the waiters at the Crown Plaza Beaverbrook Hotel restaurant. You went that extra mile offering us a table with a view of the Saint John River and serving puréed fish chowder even if it wasn't on the menu! Thank you for treating Mum like a queen.

I would like to thank my siblings who contributed in their own ways to helping my mother live on her own terms. To my brother Geoffrey Gammon and his partner Renée Losier on the home front in Fredericton... I say with gratitude—I could not have lived in peace in Berlin without knowing you were there. Geoffrey was not the cuddly type but he could always be counted on to repair a wall clock, take Mum to the cat show or show her his latest photography on his latest iPad! Renée was a step-in daughter doing what I would have loved to have done, inviting Mum for Mother's Day or Christmas. Thanks for giving Mum a family outside the home! My sister Jennifer Douglas and her husband Dan lived almost as far from Fredericton as I did, in British Columbia. They pilgrimaged home for important reunions or financially helped me make emergency trips. Jen, thanks for being there for those important "what to do now" calls. My brother Peter Gammon in St. John's, Newfoundland, our genius in the family—I can't tell you what your calls meant to Mum. No matter what mood she was in, she would rally her most intellectual self to talk with you. To my sister Jeanne Bango in Montreal—thank you for coming as often as you could and reminding Mum that you loved her.

Lastly I would like to thank Howard White and the Harbour team. Thank you Howard for recognizing that this is a very important topic—that how we live with our elders with memory loss is a litmus test of our humanity. To the Harbour Publishing team it has been a pleasure—kind, smooth, just a lovely process.

*

I am grateful that Mum gave a little warning so I could fly in the night before she died. We actually had a lovely visit that evening. I called my sister and we sang camp songs on speakerphone. Mum was still smiling and enjoying life. Then the next day around noon, Nov. 18th, 2015, I had done everything there was to do and I was relaxed and holding Mum's hand, humming along to Christmas carols when Mum just stopped breathing from one breath to the next. I had heard the expression to "die in your sleep"—well, that is how Mum died. I think Frances could die so peacefully because she had a good life right up until the end. Her village took care of her.

Oh Carolyn, you're not fifty are you?
Soon you'll be older than I am.

About the Author

Carolyn Gammon has been widely anthologized across Canada, the United States and Europe, and she is the author of *Lesbians Ignited* (Gynergy/Ragweed, 1992), *Johanna Krause Twice Persecuted: Surviving in Nazi Germany and Communist East Germany* (Wilfrid Laurier University Press, 2007) and *The Unwritten Diary of Israel Unger* (WLU Press, 2014, with Israel Unger). She was born and raised in Fredericton, New Brunswick. Her parents, Frances (Firth) Gammon and Donald Gammon, co-founded the *Fiddlehead* magazine at the University of New Brunswick. Carolyn Gammon lives in Berlin, Germany.

PHOTO CREDIT: AUTHOR-SELFIE